One World Vegetarian Cookbook

For Annie and Gabriel

Acknowledgements
Many thanks to the gardener for the supply of wonderful garden produce, William Beinart, whose green fingers are as famous as his cooking. Thanks to everyone who sent in recipes: it's been fun testing and tasting them this year. Thanks to Andy for great design, and to colleagues at the New Internationalist for their support. Lastly, special thanks to my horse Copper and her field mate Harley, for the unending supply of high-quality manure that keeps our garden in peak condition.

First published in the USA in 2011 by

INTERLINK BOOKS
An imprint of Interlink Publishing Group, Inc.
46 Crosby Street, Northampton, Massachusetts 01060
www.interlinkbooks.com

Library of Congress Cataloging-in-Publication Data available

ISBN 978-1-56656-834-0

Design by Andy Kokotka/New Internationalist

Printed and bound in China by 1010 Printing International Ltd.

To request our complete 48-page full-color catalog, please call us toll free at 1-800-238-LINK, visit our website at www.interlinkbooks.com, or send us an e-mail: info@interlinkbooks.com

FSC
Mixed Sources
Product group from well-managed forests, controlled sources and recycled wood or fibre
Cert no. SGS-COC-003963
www.fsc.org
© 1996 Forest Stewardship Council

One World Vegetarian Cookbook

by Troth Wells

Interlink Books

An imprint of Interlink Publishing Group, Inc.
Northampton, Massachusetts

STARTERS, SOUPS AND SNACKS

MAIN DISHES

MAIN DISHES – *continued*

SALADS, SIDE DISHES AND SAUCES

DESSERTS, DRINKS AND CAKES

The Global Vegetarian Kitchen

OUR SOUTH AFRICAN friend Luvuyo came to stay while I was starting work on this book. Naturally, we had a look at the veg growing in the garden, and in particular the maize. This plant, originally from Central America, is now the staple in many African countries. As we stood there in the sun, Luvuyo told me how, when he was a teenager, he used to eat a dish of maize/sweetcorn and *maas* (like yogurt) at his grandparents' place in the former Transkei. Of course I asked him for the recipe! It is included in this book, along with the story.

Luvuyo checking out our maize/sweetcorn

All photos in this section © Troth Wells

Luvuyo is not a vegetarian, but he eats less meat than he used to. For him, as with other people, this is partly because of health concerns – for example, we are more aware of the dangers of heart disease from a diet rich in meat and dairy produce. With even lean meat packing a high fat punch, it is clearly not helpful for our hearts or our waistlines.

Sadly, meat consumption is rising fastest in the Majority World, in parallel with rising wealth (for some people). The average person there now consumes nearly 30 kilograms a year, still far behind the average of about 80 kilograms a year in the rich world. The increase has been marked in China and India, whose burgeoning middle-classes are spearheading the meat boom (no doubt aided and abetted by the glitz of McDonald's, KFC et al) as global capitalism and style walk hand in hand.

While in parts of the Majority World meat is increasingly associated with status, more disposable income and with having 'made it', in other places it is a symbol of virility, something that a 'real' man has to eat. In hunting-gathering communities, which are becoming fewer by the decade, meat is central but may actually only be eaten sporadically – and the animals are not reared intensively for human consumption. It's a more sustainable, more balanced relationship.

The surge in meat consumption has required a parallel surge in grain production. Farmers now feed about 200-250 million more tonnes of grain to their animals than they did 20 years ago. This is clearly a wasteful use of resources, as Garry Peterson notes in *Ecological Economics*: 'Calorie for calorie, you need more grain if you eat it transformed into meat than if you eat it as bread: it takes three kilograms of cereals to produce a kilo of pork, eight for a kilo of beef.'

Another downside of livestock rearing is at the other end of the animal: the problem of the methane that ruminants produce. I know this is serious, but it still makes me smile. There's a kind of logic to the demise of humans being blown on the wind from a key food-source. But realizing that livestock production overall creates 80 per cent of the greenhouse-gas emissions from agriculture soon freezes the smile.

Leave animals in peace

The worst aspect is the cruelty that animals suffer before they grace our tables. Many live stunted, constrained lives, stuffed with food and drugs such

Versatile vegetable: ever popular zucchini/courgette.

as antibiotics or (in the US) growth hormones. Vast feedlots fatten up cattle before they meet their death. Chickens perch in torment on deformed feet in tiny cages. We probably would not know so much of the horror, were it not for organizations such as Compassion in World Farming, Animal Aid and People for the Ethical Treatment of Animals (PETA). The rise in organic and free-range animal production is a welcome, though flawed and incomplete, answer.

The truth is that we cannot feed the whole world with meat and dairy products. It is not sustainable, even if it were desirable. Already, 70 per cent of all agricultural land and 30 per cent of the world's surface land area is given over to livestock. That does not leave a lot to play with.

And livestock-rearing does not make good use of the land. A farmer can feed up to 30 people for a year on one hectare with vegetables, fruits, cereals and vegetable fats. But if the same area is used for the production of meat, milk or eggs, the number of persons fed falls to between 5 and 10.

So, eating animals is not good for us; it is certainly not good for them, and it is helping to destroy the planet. We have to look elsewhere for food.

And this is where it gets so interesting and everything becomes possible – there are lots of bright spots in this firmament. For example, it is noticeable that dishes without meat are much more widely available than they used to be. When I lived in Malaysia in the 1980s, there were few restaurants that styled themselves 'vegetarian' as such – although of course much of the Indian cuisine there did not contain meat. But on a recent visit to Penang, I noticed that several places now advertised themselves as vegetarian. Clearly this is in part for the tourist market, but nonetheless it is an important change.

What's in a name?

The numbers of people who call themselves vegetarian or vegan are not huge. Vegetarians and vegans remain a small minority. In Britain a November 2007 survey by the Department of Environment, Farming and Rural Affairs showed two per cent to be vegan, three per cent vegetarian and a further five per cent restricting

More visibility for veggies in Malaysia.

themselves to fish or chicken. In other Western countries vegetarians and vegans are an even smaller minority.

But perhaps people do not like being labeled, or to even to label themselves. Or maybe some of the evangelizing steam has gone out of vegetarianism as a movement. My sense is that people don't feel the need so much to proclaim their vegetarian credentials because non-meat foods are so much more available, and they are more central in our lives and on our plates. The vegetables and plant foods on offer are so plentiful and varied, so much more fun and interesting, that eating them has become mainstream in a way that was hard to contemplate some years back.

For lots of people, the days are gone when a plate without meat is seen as deficient. In the rich world, and for richer people in the Majority World, there is a wealth of attractive, fresh, crisp, colorful, satisfying, zingy things to eat. Market stalls groan with red peppers and fleshy round tomatoes, frilly green lettuces, cheeky pink radishes, cool cukes, the purple promise of eggplants/aubergines, serried ranks of corn on the cob, knobbly potatoes, velvety mushrooms, zucchini/courgettes lying sleekly, rich ruby soft fruits offsetting the acid yellow of lemons, sacks of red lentils and white rice, piles of spices and bundles of herbs... What a kaleidoscope of shapes, sizes, colors and textures.

For a lot of us, that market may reside in a supermarket, even though we might prefer to be like food writer Nigel Slater who has 'honestly never set foot inside a branch of Tesco' and mainly shops at 'small local shops, farmers' markets, proper butchers, fishmongers, delicatessens and cheese shops rather than all at once on a weekly trip to a supermarket'. Oh well! We can but try, and do what we can.

Grow your own

Growing your own vegetables is another part of the picture, for what is more enticing than planting seeds and watching them transform into delicious food for your table? Even if you do not have a garden, you can probably manage to grow a little parsley or other herbs in a pot. It is rewarding – good for the soul as well as the body. And while we won't grow enough to fully feed ourselves, it is a start. Barbara Kingsolver, best-selling author of *The Poisonwood Bible*, upped sticks for the farming life with her family. They had a farm in the Appalachian mountains, and spent a fun year growing everything and rearing some animals too. She wrote amusingly about it in her book *Animal, Vegetable, Miracle*. As she says, 'Many of us who aren't farmers or gardeners still

Young plants stretch towards the sun.

have some element of farm nostalgia in our family past'.

Over the course of this last year, while preparing this book, I have looked at our garden with renewed enthusiasm. Seeing the brave overwintering plants under a coating of snow, and then later the first seedling mavericks trying their luck against weather and slugs, to the end of summer when raspberries, sweetcorn, apples, pears, carrots, potatoes, zucchini/courgettes, peppers, eggplant/ aubergines, tomatoes and various herbs are in abundance. There is something deeply satisfying about being in physical touch with the soil and making your own food out of what you grow.

Earlier **New Internationalist** food books focused entirely on Majority World recipes and in their way, I hope, have done a little to raise awareness

Penny's Aussie Pavlova.

of the great foods that people cook wherever they live and whatever difficulties they have to endure. The idea of this book is rather different. It really begins in my garden – or your windowbox, allotment, yard or small pot of parsley. The little seed of the idea is this: no matter how good or hopeless you may be at growing

Summer delight: garden peas.

Gooseberry jam – tart, tantalising taste.

things, you can probably manage something. And that is a start. I'm not great at vegetable gardening, nor a star cook by any means, but that doesn't stop me enjoying what I do. Some of the things in the book are made from just what was in the garden at the time, such as parsnips and fennel turned into soup. Or elderflower cordial brewed from the fragrant heavy blooms in June that covered the bushes in the field where my old horse, Copper, lives. Such recipes are pretty easy, but they taste good. And I guess for a lot of people, that is what matters.

Moving on from my – or your – home, the recipes then reach around the world. Most were kindly sent in by friends, and friends of the **New Internationalist**. They are from a range of countries, including Europe, North America and Australasia. You'll find familiar classics such as lasagna, nut roast, Boston baked beans, and an Aussie Pavlova that will have you begging for more.

And, to continue in our **New Internationalist** food book tradition, most of the recipes come from Africa, India, China, other parts of Asia, the Middle East and Latin America – including a tasty South African bean *bredie* or stew, rich couscous from Morocco, the wonderfully named 'Bibimbap' veg and rice dish from Korea, Nepalese lentil curry, lemon-grass scented Thai soup, spicy eggplant/aubergine from Indonesia, crunchy garlicky potatoes from India, Mexican burritos, and a papaya/pawpaw dessert from Brazil... not to mention a dreamy Cuban daiquiri to sip while cooking, perhaps. There's a diversity and delight of vegetarian foods for you to cook in your kitchen – and to enjoy at your table!

Troth Wells

Notes to the recipes

Most of the recipes are vegan or are vegan-adaptable by using soy margarine, milk or yogurt. For green herbs, the quantities in the recipes are for fresh herbs, which give better flavor. But using dried herbs is fine if you cannot get fresh; you would normally use a smaller amount – 1 tbsp (tablespoon) of fresh parsley would be about 1 tsp (teaspoon) of dried.

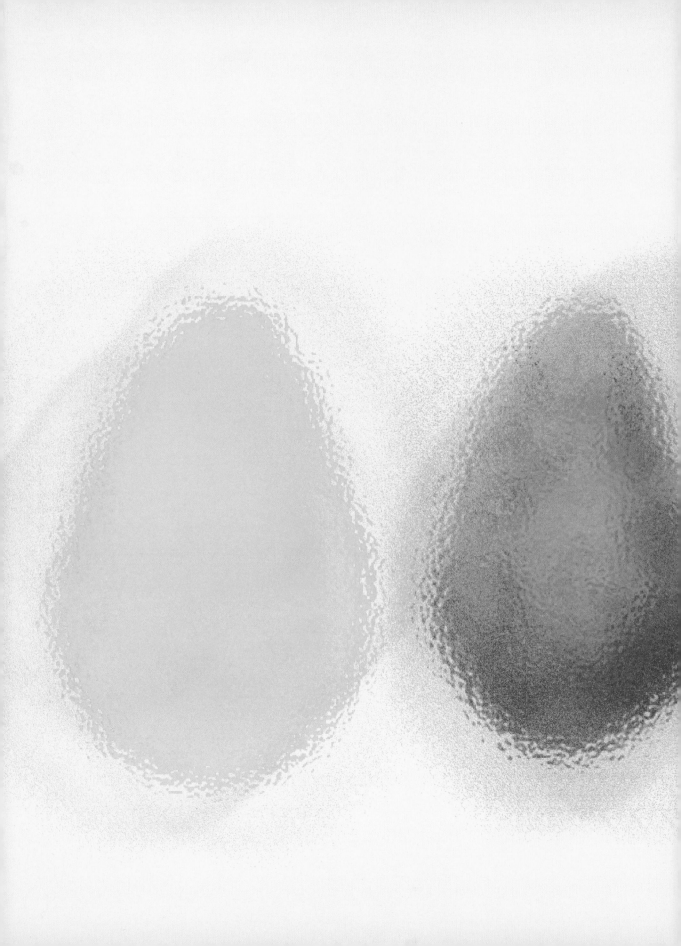

STARTERS, SOUPS AND SNACKS

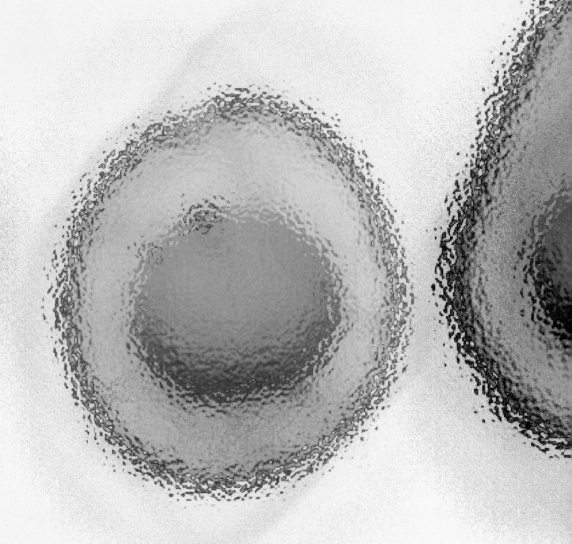

Baba ghanoush
– eggplant/aubergine dip

The favorite eggplant/aubergine *mezze* dip has a good flavor, emphasized by the tahini. You can serve with pita bread and chopped vegetable sticks such as carrots, peppers and cucumber.

SERVES 4

Preparation: 15 minutes
Cooking: 15 minutes

2 eggplants/aubergines

2 cloves garlic

¼ tsp ground cumin

¼ tsp ground coriander

2 tbsp lemon juice

1 tbsp tahini

1 tbsp yogurt or oil

1 tbsp parsley, chopped

oil

salt and pepper

paalia under a CC License

1 Prick the eggplants/aubergines with a skewer or fork. Heat the grill and when it is hot, put the eggplants under. Turn them from time to time and cook until they are soft. Remove and set aside to cool. When cool, scoop out pulp and chop.

2 Now place the eggplants/aubergines into a blender and add the garlic, cumin and coriander, lemon juice, tahini, seasoning and yogurt or oil. You may need to do this in batches. Add more juice, yogurt or oil to make the consistency you require.

3 Spoon into a dish and scatter the parsley on top before serving.

Besara - bean dip

This is our version of a Middle Eastern broad bean dip. Large dried broad beans (*ful nabed*), also called fava beans, are often used for Besara. But you can use fresh, frozen or tinned beans of other varieties too.

SERVES 4 - 6

Preparation: 5 minutes
Cooking: 5 minutes

3 cups / 225 g beans, cooked

2 tbsp mint, chopped

1 tbsp yogurt

olive oil

1 tbsp lemon juice

1 lemon, cut into wedges

salt and pepper

1 Purée the beans and then place them in a bowl. Add the mint, yogurt, lemon juice and olive oil to make a dressing. Season.

2 Serve with hot pita bread, and have olive oil and lemon wedges to hand round.

Ahron de Leeuw under a CC License

Butternut squash soup

A firm family favorite – with a lovely warm color too. Butternuts are easy to peel with a carrot peeler or sharp knife and for this recipe you cut off the bottom as well. Good with warm, crunchy bread.
Helen Beinart, Oxford, England

SERVES 4

Preparation: 10 minutes
Cooking: 45 minutes

1 tsp cumin seeds

1 onion, chopped

2 cloves garlic, crushed

1 leek, sliced

3-pound / 1.5-kg butternut squash, peeled, halved and de-seeded

1½ quarts / 1.5 liters stock

2 tbsp parsley, chopped

2-4 tbsp crème fraîche or yogurt

oil

salt and pepper

1 To begin, heat some oil in a large pan and lightly toast the cumin seeds.

2 After a couple of minutes, add the onion, garlic, leek and the butternut squash.

3 Cover the pan and sweat on a low heat for 15-20 minutes. Shake or stir the pot from time to time to prevent sticking.

4 Pour in the stock to cover the vegetables and cook for 30 minutes or until tender. Leave to cool. Roughly chop the squash in the pan with a knife.

5 Whiz the soup with a hand-held blender; season. Then stir in the crème fraîche or yogurt and warm through gently. Add some chopped parsley before serving with warm, crunchy bread.

Caponata – eggplant/aubergine antipasto

SERVES 6

*Preparation: 2-3 hours
(includes soaking time for
eggplants/aubergines*)
Cooking: 30 minutes*

4 eggplants/aubergines,
  diced

1 cup / 150 g pitted green
  olives, roughly chopped

1 tbsp capers

2 sticks celery, sliced

2-3 onions, finely diced

2 cans tomatoes

½ cup / 120 ml red wine
  vinegar

1 tbsp brown sugar

3 tbsp basil leaves,
  chopped

1 tbsp salt *

oil

salt and pepper

* Soaking the eggplants/
aubergines in salted water
removes any bitterness but it also
means that they do not soak up
so much oil when cooking. If you
prefer not to do this, omit #1.

This is a Sicilian dish served as part of an array of antipasti, and using local olive oil. It's my favorite antipasto, and is usually served along with cold salamis and bruschetta but can easily be served on its own. Good caponata requires love and time and is a great dish to do when you have an afternoon to yourself to potter around the kitchen. This recipe below, based on one by Eufemia Azzolina Pupella, makes quite a bit – certainly enough to serve six people as an antipasto and then the rest you can either freeze or take round to friends as a pleasant surprise… along with a bottle, of course!
Annie Tiranti, London, England

1 Place the eggplants/aubergines into water with the tablespoon of salt dissolved; you may need several bowls to fit in all the eggplant/aubergines. Leave for 2 hours. If not soaking, go to #2.

2 Heat some oil in a large pan and fry the eggplant/aubergine (you may need to do this in batches) for about 20 minutes, until they are soft and brown.

3 Place the capers in a bowl of hot water for few minutes to draw out the salt; drain.

4 Boil some water and parboil the celery for 3-5 minutes to soften; then drain.

5 Place the onions with a splash of olive

oil in a very large saucepan, on a low heat. Add the capers, olives and celery and mix together. Stir in the tomatoes, gently breaking them up. Let this all simmer slowly for about 30 minutes.

6 Meanwhile, if you have soaked the eggplants/aubergines, now take them out and dry them carefully – laying them on a clean tea towel and then drawing all four corners of the tea towel together to make a loose ball and gently shaking works well. Using a fresh pan, heat some olive oil, and fry them in batches, adding more oil as necessary.

7 Once all the eggplants/aubergines are cooked and nicely browned, place them into the sauce mixture (this is why you need the large saucepan!). Add the sugar and vinegar, 1 tbsp of the basil leaves; mix together and season to taste. The sauce should be reduced and thicker by now. Continue to simmer gently for 10 minutes to combine the flavors.

8 Turn off the heat and cover, allowing the caponata to cool. Serve cold in a bowl with the remaining basil leaves scattered on top. You can either eat as it is, or place on crackers or crusty bread.

Corn-on-the-cob in coconut milk

This is a poor person's meal which is very popular in Tanzania. It is cheap and readily available everywhere. It is also very tasty. It is better than it sounds and my friends can never have enough of it.
Kamar Goddard, England

SERVES 4

Preparation: 5 minutes
Cooking: 25 minutes

8 x 3-inch/8-cm pieces of sweetcorn

1¼ cups / 300 ml coconut milk

pinch turmeric

juice of 1 lemon

1 tbsp cilantro/coriander, chopped

salt

1 Put the coconut milk, turmeric and lemon juice into a saucepan. Bring to a gentle boil, stirring all the time.

2 Now put in the corn cobs and simmer very gently for 20 minutes or until the corn is tender. Now add the cilantro/coriander and simmer for a further 2 minutes. Season.

3 Serve with skewers or forks at each end, and drizzle with the sauce.

brockzilla under a CC License

Dutch pea soup

This homemade soup has been passed on from mother to daughter to grand-daughter. Pea soup (also called *snert*) is a popular winter soup in the Netherlands. Almost every area has its own version. It is served with a thick slice of homemade bread on a cold wintry evening... and if you can leave it, the soup tastes even better the next day.

Henriette Faber, Kelowna, British Columbia, Canada

SERVES 8-12

Preparation: 10 minutes
Cooking: 45 minutes

2½ quarts / 2.5 liters water

2¼ cups / 490 g green split peas

2 leeks, chopped finely

1 stick celery, chopped finely

1 carrot, sliced finely

1 potato, diced

4 bouillon/stock cubes

1 bay leaf

salt and pepper

1 In a heavy pan or Dutch oven, bring the water to a boil. When it's boiling, add all the other ingredients, except the salt and pepper.

2 Simmer, covered, for 45 minutes to 1 hour or until the vegetables are done – stir from time to time. Add salt and pepper to taste. Serve with homemade bread.

zwolle under a CC License

Gazpacho

One of our summer favorites based on the popular Spanish soup – a lovely way to use home-grown cucumbers, tomatoes, onions, garlic and parsley… and sometimes the bell peppers grow big enough too! Apparently, traditional Andalusian gazpacho does not include tomatoes because they are not native to Spain. But when I had this first, in Sevilla in 1968, it certainly looked as if it had tomatoes in it. Oh, and there were two large prawns and a slice of lemon perched on the edge of the glass in which it was served. Quite a sight, and a taste, for someone more accustomed to Heinz tomato soup, as many of us were in those days!

SERVES 4

Preparation: 15 minutes

1-2 slices bread

1 onion, sliced

3 cloves garlic, crushed

12-inch/30-cm cucumber, sliced

1-2 red bell peppers

8-12 tomatoes, chopped

3 tbsp red wine or sherry

2 cups / 490 ml water or vegetable juice

juice of 1 lemon

½ tsp paprika

3 tbsp olive oil

3 tbsp parsley, chopped

salt and pepper

1 Soak the bread in water and then squeeze out the excess moisture.

2 Then place it in the blender with all the other ingredients and whiz (you may need to do this in a couple of batches).

3 When ready, adjust seasoning and then leave to chill in the fridge for a couple of hours before serving with the parsley on top.

Greek cheese pies

Street vendors in Athens were selling these deep-fried goodies.
The taste was delicious and as vegetarian campers we had been
mainly cooking our own food.

We eat them regularly at home and are instantly transported
back to the streets of Greece.

Jan Lancaster

MAKES 12

Preparation: 15 minutes
Cooking: 5 minutes

1-2 tbsp butter or margarine

3 filo pastry sheets

2 cups / 250 g feta cheese

1 small tub cottage cheese

½ cup yogurt

2 tbsp plain flour

1 egg

1-2 cloves garlic, chopped

½ tsp nutmeg, grated

**1 tbsp parsley or cilantro/
coriander, chopped**

1 tsp sesame seeds

peanut oil

1 Melt the butter or margarine in a
pan. When melted, brush onto the filo
pastry sheets.

2 Mix together the feta and cottage
cheese, the yogurt, flour, egg, garlic,
nutmeg and herbs.

3 Spoon onto a sheet of buttered
filo pastry, fold into a rectangular
shape, and then cut into pieces about
1½-inches/4-cms square. Top with
sesame seeds.

4 Heat some peanut oil in a pan and
when hot, fry the pies for a couple of
minutes on both sides (don't let them
burn) and then drain on kitchen towel
and serve hot.

Harira – spicy bean soup

When I was staying in Marrakesh, the *diffa,* or feast, comprising many courses was served one night. There were several meat dishes, so I asked if I could eat only non-meat ones. They were happy for that, and charged very little – perhaps because the meat dishes were the centerpiece. This bean soup, Harira, is often made with lamb but this is a meatless version. I sometimes add peas or other veg to use them up.

SERVES 6

Preparation: 15 minutes
Cooking: 30 minutes

1 onion, chopped

1 can garbanzos/chickpeas

1 can white kidney or
  borlotti beans

1 can tomatoes

½ tsp saffron threads

½ tsp cinnamon

¼ green chili, de-seeded
  and chopped or ¼ tsp
  chili powder

2 tbsp cilantro/coriander,
  chopped

2 tbsp parsley, chopped

juice of 1 lemon

2 quarts / 2 liters stock

½ cup / 100 g rice

1 tbsp flour

oil

salt and pepper

1 Using a saucepan, gently fry the onion and then add the garbanzos/chickpeas, beans, tomatoes, saffron, cinnamon and chili/powder.

2 Then put in one tablespoon of the parsley plus the cilantro/coriander, the lemon juice and seasoning. Stir well and cook for 5 minutes.

3 Now pour in the stock and then add the rice. Stir well, and boil for 10-15 minutes until the rice is soft.

4 While that is cooking, mix the flour with a little water to make a roux and stir this into the soup.

5 Adjust the seasonings, and cook for a further 15 minutes, stirring from time to time. Serve with the remaining parsley on top.

Fran Harvey

Hearty cabbage soup

Here is a recipe for soup which I use every week in the winter months. It's a quick, tasty and cheap meal when I come home from looking after Harley and Copper (horses, who provide excellent manure for lots of local gardens!).

I had thought the soup might conjure up images of diets and that infamous cabbage smell – but this is great! Lovely and creamy. My grandson came back for third helpings, which is usually unheard of...

Glynis Coxeter, Oxford, England

SERVES 4

Preparation: 10 minutes
Cooking: 25 minutes

1 onion, sliced

3 cloves garlic, chopped

1 pound / 450 g potatoes, chopped into small chunks

1 quart / 1 liter vegetable bouillon/stock

1 tbsp parsley, chopped

1 savoy cabbage, chopped

1 can cannelloni beans, butter beans or sweetcorn [+]

oil

salt and pepper

[+] optional

1 Sauté the onion until soft and then add the garlic.

2 Now add the potatoes and fry gently for about 5 minutes.

3 After that, pour in the stock and sprinkle in the parsley, stir, and simmer for 10 minutes or until the potatoes begin to soften.

4 Next, put in the cabbage, and the beans or sweetcorn if using. Bring to the boil and simmer for about 20 minutes, stirring occasionally.

5 When ready, liquidize (adding more bouillon/stock or water if necessary) and then season. Heat through and serve with crusty bread and crumbled stilton or cheddar cheese on the top.

STARTERS, SOUPS & SNACKS   35

Hummus...

...with red bell pepper

There are many ways to prepare hummus, with different flavorings.
So feel free to experiment. This version is popular in our household.

1 Start by heating the oil and then cook the red pepper strips. When they are soft, keep a few to one side for decoration.

2 Now put all the ingredients into a food processor – depending on its capacity you may need to do several batches – and whiz to make a smoothish consistency. Adjust the flavors to suit your taste, and then pour or spoon the hummus into a dish and decorate with the retained red pepper strips before serving.

SERVES 4

Preparation: 10 minutes
Cooking: 5 minutes

1 red bell pepper, cut into strips

2 cups / 400 g can garbanzos/ chickpeas

2-3 cloves garlic

2-3 tsp tahini

1-2 tbsp lemon juice

1-2 tbsp yogurt [+]

pinch of paprika

oil

salt and pepper

[+] optional – if not using, adjust the consistency by adding more lemon juice and/or oil.

...with spices

Some like it hot… chili gives a tang to the warm blandness, giving a surprise. I made this without tahini as I found we didn't have any, and thought I'd use sesame seeds instead. It tasted good.

1 Put all the ingredients into a food processor and whiz to make a creamy texture. You may need to do several batches. Use more yogurt, oil and/or lemon juice to get the consistency you prefer.

2 Adjust the flavors to suit your taste, then spoon the hummus into a dish and sprinkle the parsley and a little more paprika on top before serving.

SERVES 4

Preparation: 10 minutes

2 cups / 400 g can garbanzos/ chickpeas

2-3 cloves garlic

1 tbsp sesame seeds or 2 tsp tahini

pinch of chili powder

½ tsp paprika

1-2 tbsp lemon juice

2 tbsp yogurt [+]

1 tbsp parsley, chopped

oil

salt and pepper

[+] optional – if not using, adjust the consistency by adding more lemon juice and/or oil.

...with cilantro/coriander and lime

Hummus is good for many occasions, and this is one with a delicate flavor; lime and cilantro/coriander is a great combination. Some people add a pinch of chili for extra zing.

1 Put all the ingredients, except one tablespoon of the cilantro/coriander, into a food processor and blend to a smooth paste. If not using yogurt, add more oil and/or lime juice.

2 Adjust the flavors to suit your taste, and then pour or spoon the hummus into a dish and top with the remaining cilantro/coriander.

<u>S E R V E S 4</u>

Preparation: 10 minutes

1 can garbanzos/chickpeas

2-3 cloves garlic

2-3 tsp tahini

1-2 tbsp lime juice

1-2 tbsp yogurt [+]

grated zest and juice of 1 lime

1-2 tbsp cilantro/coriander, chopped

oil

salt and pepper

[+] optional – if not using, adjust the consistency by adding more lemon juice and/or oil.

Moroccan spicy olives

Ideally you should leave the olives in their marinade overnight,
or for several hours, shaking or stirring them from time to time,
to let the flavors expand.

SERVES 4-6

Preparation: 5 minutes
Cooking: 2 minutes

1 tsp cumin seeds

1 tsp fennel seeds

1 tsp coriander seeds

½ tsp ground cardamom

a pinch of chili powder

¼ tsp ground nutmeg

¼ tsp cinnamon

1 tbsp olive oil

1½ cups / 225 g green olives

3-4 cloves garlic, crushed

1 tbsp lemon juice

lemon rind/zest, thinly pared

1 tbsp orange juice

1 Heat the olive oil and then gently toast the seeds, cardamom, chili, nutmeg and cinnamon for a few minutes.

2 Now transfer to a bowl and add the olives, garlic, juices and lemon zest. Toss to coat evenly.

3 Cover the bowl, or place in an airtight container in the fridge to let the marinade penetrate fully.

c.hug under a CC License

Orzotto
– creamy barley risotto

This dish of barley in a creamy sauce is a typical recipe of my country area, Friuli, a region near Venice. It is simple, and well balanced from a nutritional standpoint.
Adriana De Zorzi, Udine, Italy

SERVES 4

Preparation: 12 hours + 15 minutes
Cooking: 45 minutes

1 cup / 200 g pearl barley, soaked for 12 hours

1 onion, chopped

1 clove garlic, chopped

1 stalk celery, chopped finely

1 carrot, chopped finely

5 cups / 1 liter vegetable bouillon/stock

1½ cups / 225 g peas

1 tbsp butter

4 tbsp parmesan or hard cheese *

oil

pepper

* Parmesan always contains rennet, but there are vegetarian hard cheeses that can be used as an equivalent.

1 Using a heavy flameproof dish, pour in the olive oil. Cook the onion and then add the garlic. Add the celery and carrot and fry gently until they are light brown.

2 Drain the barley, and put it into the pan with the vegetables. Pour in the bouillon/stock, stirring to mix well. Cover and bring to the boil, then reduce the heat and simmer for 20 minutes. Now put in the peas.

3 Continue to cook for a further 15-20 minutes and, just before you serve, add the butter, pepper (you may not need salt) and cheese. Stir again, and serve with crusty bread.

House of Sims under a CC license

Palta rellena - avocado stuffed with mixed vegetables

I have a fascination with Peruvian foods. I've worked with many vegetarians in Peru, where not eating meat is almost unheard of ('vegetarian' dishes have been seen including chicken or fish). But if you're not vegan, there are lots of options if you know what to look for.
Abby Shuler

SERVES 8

Preparation: 10 minutes
Cooking: 10 minutes

4 avocados, cut in half

2 cups / 300 g peas

2 carrots, diced/cubed

4 potatoes, diced and boiled

8 lettuce leaves

4 cooked eggs, sliced

mayonnaise

salt and pepper

1 Mix the mayonnaise with the cooked potatoes, carrots and peas. Add salt and pepper to taste. Now pile the mix into the avocados.

2 Arrange the lettuce leaves on a plate and place the avocados on them. Decorate with the egg slices and serve.

Theodore Scott under a CC License

Parsnip and apple soup

Another great warming soup, and the apples give a
gentle tartness as a pleasant counterpoint to the parsnip.

SERVES 4

Preparation: 10 minutes
Cooking: 30 minutes

1 parsnip, chopped

1-2 apples, chopped

1 onion, sliced

1 tbsp fennel root or stem,
  chopped

1 potato, chopped

1½ cups / 360 ml bouillon/stock

1½ cups / 360 ml milk

1 tbsp fennel fronds, chopped

oil

salt and pepper

1 To start, fry the onion until it
is soft. Then put in the parsnip,
apple, fennel root or stem and
potato.

2 Next, pour in the stock, bring
to the boil and simmer for 15-20
minutes until the vegetables are
soft. Leave to cool a little.

3 When ready, blend the
vegetables and stock, adding milk
or water to make the consistency
you prefer. Season, and then serve
hot, decorated with the chopped
fennel fronds.

STARTERS, SOUPS & SNACKS   45

Ribollita – thick Tuscan soup

A filling, hearty soup-stew from the Tuscany area of Italy. Ribollita means 're-boiled' or cooked again, and certainly it gets better if you can leave it for a couple of hours before reheating. I first ate this in a market in Florence, sitting on a rickety stool by a trader's stall. It was what the market vendors and workers were eating; good, filling soup which is often made from left-overs. When I revisited Florence a few years ago, this seemed to be served in many mainstream restaurants at lunchtime.

SERVES 6

Preparation time: 20 minutes
(+ 2 hours if possible)
Cooking time: 30 minutes
(+ additional 30 minutes to reheat)

1 onion, sliced

3 cloves garlic, sliced

2 carrots, chopped

3 potatoes, chopped

1-2 sticks celery, chopped

1 leek, sliced

2-4 zucchini/courgettes, sliced

1 can borlotti beans

1 can tomatoes

1 savoy cabbage, sliced

1 pound / 450 g spinach or kale, chopped +

1 quart / 1 liter bouillon/stock or water

3 tbsp tomato paste/purée

2-4 slices stale bread or 1 ciabatta

2 tbsp parsley, chopped

grated cheddar

oil

salt and pepper

+ optional

1 Sauté the onion in a large pan, and when it is golden add the garlic. Adding more oil if necessary, now put in the other vegetables except the beans, tomatoes, cabbage and spinach or kale.

2 Stir the pot and then cover and let the ingredients cook gently on a low heat for 10 minutes or so.

3 Now put in the beans, tomatoes, tomato paste/purée, cabbage and spinach or kale. Pour in the bouillon/stock or water to cover the vegetables and bring to the boil. Season, then simmer for 20 minutes or until the potatoes and carrot are softening. You can partially mash the ingredients if you wish, using a potato masher or a wooden spoon.

4 Break the bread into the soup, ensuring it is well absorbed. Add more water if necessary. Now, if you can leave the soup to stand for a couple of hours or longer, this allows the flavors to expand and the soup ingredients to merge. Reheat gently and scatter on the parsley and grated cheese before serving.

Skordalia me karydia – walnut and bread dip

I'm usually very good at being able to copy a dish once I've had it. But I spent ages with a Greek waiter in a little taverna trying to work out what was in this first dip – he kept pointing to the trees and holding up pine cones! After some help from Denise's Greek relatives we realized he was trying to describe walnuts. I had been convinced that it wasn't vegetarian/vegan and that I might have been eating little birds nesting next to the pine cones in the trees… The bread, walnuts and vinegar mixture give it a really different taste.

Michael York and Denise Salambasis, Oxford, England

SERVES 4-6
Preparation: 5 minutes

3 cups / 150 g old bread, broken up, soaked in water for a couple of minutes, and then squeezed to remove excess water

2-8 cloves garlic, crushed

1¼ cups / 300 ml olive oil

1¼ cups / 150 g walnuts, grated or broken up

⅓ cup / 75 ml wine vinegar

salt

1 Put the bread and garlic in a bowl with the salt and mix. Then gradually add the oil, nuts and vinegar. If it's too thick you can add a little warm water.

2 This is quite a lumpy dip if you make it by hand but you can use a processor and make it smooth. It's great served cold, with fried zucchini/courgettes and eggplants/aubergines.

Tahini dip

A Greek recipe that is popular in our family.
Michael York and Denise Salambasis, Oxford, England

SERVES 4
Preparation: 5 minutes

juice of 1 lemon

2 cloves garlic, crushed

3 tbsp parsley, finely chopped

½ cup / 110 g tahini

salt

Mix all the ingredients together. You can serve this with toast or on a plain salad, or with carrot sticks, crisps and so on.

Sort-of French onion soup

This is traditionally made with chicken stock, but vegetable stock with a bit of yeast extract such as Marmite or Vegemite added is fine. For a more substantial meal, serve with toasted cheese on the side. If you can leave the soup after cooking it, and then reheat it later, it helps develop the flavor.

SERVES 4

Preparation: 10 minutes
Cooking: 70 minutes

2 onions, sliced finely into rings

2 cloves garlic, crushed

1-1½ tsp yeast extract

1 quart / 1 liter bouillon/stock

1 cup / 240 ml red wine

1 tbsp parsley, chopped

½-1 tsp sugar [+]

oil

pepper

[+] optional

1 Sauté the onions in a heavy pan, over a gentle heat. When they are soft, add the garlic and stir round. Then pour in a little stock to cover them and continue to cook for 5 minutes.

2 Pour in the remaining stock and add the yeast extract to taste. Now add the wine, and the sugar if using. Season with pepper (you may not need salt), and then cook, covered, for an hour. Serve with the parsley scattered on top. You can also use croutons.

Spanish omelet

When I was a student at Madrid University back in the 1960s, Spanish omelet was a great snack – I ate it many times when I lived there later when working for the Bank of London and South America. I didn't stay long at the Bank, not my scene really, but I fell in love with Spain and still teach Spanish. And of course I love the food – Spanish omelet being one of my earliest and easiest things to cook. The classic Spanish omelet, a popular tapas or snack, is just eggs, potatoes and onions, seasoned with salt and pepper, and fried in oil. Once it is cooked on one side, you place a plate over the pan, turn the whole thing over and then slide the omelet back into the pan the other way up – takes quite a lot of skill to do this!

David Wells-Cole, Leatherhead, Surrey, England

1 onion, sliced finely
2 potatoes, diced and cooked
4 eggs, beaten
salt and pepper
oil

1 Heat some oil and gently cook the onion until it is soft and beginning to caramelize (don't let it burn).

2 Then put in the potatoes. Heat them through and season.

3 Now, with the pan hot, pour in the beaten eggs and gently pull back the omelet from the sides as it forms so that all the egg cooks.

4 When brown on the underside, place a plate over the pan and carefully turn the pan over so that the omelet is on the plate, browned side up. Now slide the omelet back into the pan, with the browned side still on top, so that the underside can cook. Serve at once, cut into wedges. It can also be served cold.

Tamia
– falafel

Tamia are similar to falafel. An easy recipe for this great snack or *mezze*/appetizer that is probably as popular in the West as in the Middle East where it originated.

MAKES 24

Preparation: 20 minutes
Cooking time: 5 minutes

1 can garbanzos/chickpeas

2-4 cloves garlic

1 onion

1 green bell pepper, chopped

1 tsp coriander seeds

2 tbsp cilantro/coriander, chopped

juice of ½ lemon

1 slice bread

2 tbsp flour

1 tsp sesame seeds + 1 tbsp sesame seeds

1 tsp baking powder

oil

salt and pepper

1 Drain the garbanzos/chickpeas and put them in a blender with the garlic, onion, bell pepper, coriander seeds and cilantro/coriander.

2 Pour the lemon juice on a plate and soak the bread in it; then squeeze out any excess liquid. Crumble the bread into the mixture.

3 Stir or blend again, then add flour, the teaspoon of sesame seeds, salt and pepper. Set aside for 10 minutes.

4 When ready, add the baking powder and mix it in well. Adjust the flavoring and seasoning to taste.

5 Take up small amounts and shape with your hands into flattish rounds. Scatter the remaining tablespoon of sesame seeds on the patties and then fry these for 2-3 minutes on each side until lightly browned. Serve with pita bread, salad and yogurt.

Julien Harneis under a CC License

Tom ka-gai
– Thai soup

This Thai soup is fragrant rather than blow-your-head-off-hot like the popular Tom Yam. It is traditionally made with chicken, but I find that mushrooms work very well instead. Ordinary mushrooms are fine, but you may prefer to use shiitake or other East Asian ones instead. If you leave the chili intact, it is not so burning, but imparts a hot and smoky tone. Galangal, also called Laos powder, is an edible rhizome that looks like ginger root. It has a lemony and peppery but earthy flavor. You can buy it in specialty shops, but if you do not locate it then use fresh ginger.

SERVES 4

Preparation: 20 minutes
Cooking: 30 minutes

2 scallions/shallots, sliced
 very finely

1 cup / 125 g mushrooms, very
 thinly sliced

1 stick lemon grass

1 lime, juice and grated peel

3-4 kaffir lime leaves

½ inch piece galangal or ginger,
 sliced finely

1 red chili, de-seeded and chopped *

2 cups / 400 ml coconut milk

1 cup / 240 ml water

1 tbsp cilantro/coriander, chopped

oil

salt

* There are many different types of chili
but the one normally used would be the
small 'bird's eye' one. If you do not like hot
things, do not cut the chili but leave it whole
for a gentler flavor.

1 In a pan, heat a little oil and sauté the scallions/shallots. Then add the mushrooms and cook them to soften.

2 Next, put in the lemon grass, grated lime peel, kaffir lime leaves, galangal or ginger, and chili. Stir and cook to blend the flavors.

3 Now pour in the coconut milk and water; stir well. Bring the soup to a simmer and cook for 10 minutes. Add the lime juice and salt; adjust the flavors and then continue to cook for a further 10 minutes.

4 Remove from heat and serve immediately, garnished with the cilantro/coriander.

Turkish thick lentil soup

I had this at the home of friends who go to Turkey quite often. The taste and richness of the soup is lovely; it is very filling, cheap and easy to make. Adding cumin and chili is my own experiment and it enhances the flavor. Wash the lentils first.

Kamar Goddard, England

SERVES 4

Preparation: 5 minutes
Cooking: 20 minutes

1 onion, sliced

3 cloves garlic, chopped

1½ cups / 300 g red lentils

1 tbsp tomato paste/purée

½-1 tsp cumin powder

¼-½ tsp chili powder

3 cups / 720 ml water

1 bouillon/stock cube

salt and pepper

1 Cook the onion in a little oil in a large pan until soft but not brown.

2 Add the garlic, lentils, tomato paste/purée, cumin and chili. Stir round to mix.

3 Dissolve the bouillon/stock cube in the water and add this to the pan. Stir well.

4 Simmer the soup until the lentils are fluffy. You can either leave the soup as it is, or blend it. Adjust the seasoning and serve.

shadiworks under a CC License

Umpotulo naMasi – corn/maize and *maas*/yogurt

I used to eat this when visiting my mother's family in Umzimkulu (formerly in Transkei, but now in KwaZulu Natal). The dish is often served at lunchtime on hot days. It's filling and quite rich but very tasty. Umzimkulu household gardens would usually grow maize in summer (November to February), harvesting in April or May – and this is when we would eat this dish. Then the cattle graze the corn stalks in winter. Many households had dairy cattle (some up to 15 cattle) and made the *maas* (curd, soured milk like yogurt) at home. I used to milk the cows when I was a boy – it's hard work and my fingers were sore! This dish makes a good snack, or a substantial appetizer.

Luvuyo Wotshela, Fort Beaufort, South Africa

Preparation: 10 minutes
Cooking: 10 minutes

per person:
1 sweetcorn cob
½ cup / 120 ml Greek yogurt
a little salt

1 Boil the sweetcorn in water for a few minutes until the kernels are tender. Drain and set aside to cool.

2 Then using your fingers, rub off the kernels into a small deep mixing bowl. Use a knife if you find it hard to remove them with your fingers. Lightly crush the kernels with a wooden spoon or the end of a rolling pin.

3 Next, season as required and spoon into a small individual dish for serving. Add the yogurt in a thick layer on top and serve cold.

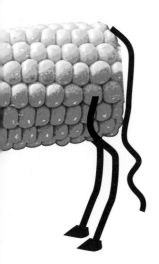

Andrew Kokotka

STARTERS, SOUPS & SNACKS   61

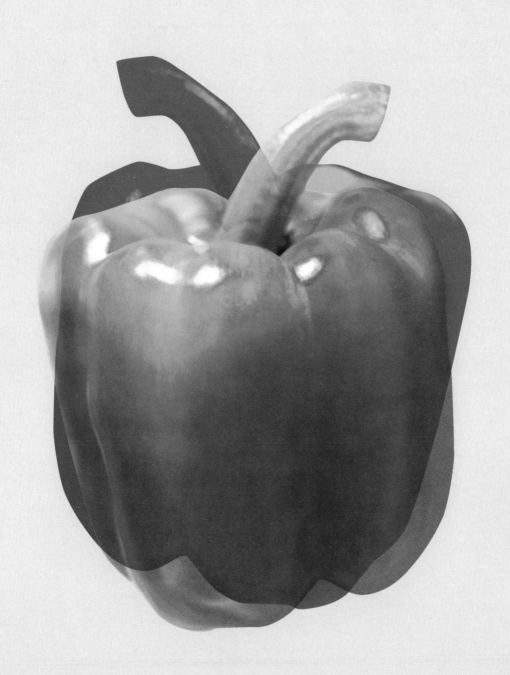

MAIN DISHES

Angel hair pasta with caramelized onions

Capellini or angel hair pasta is fine like… angel's hair. This entrée was created by a friend who had a similar meal in a Greek/Italian diner, and recreated it at home. The onions are sweet, the feta is a bit tart, and the pasta is the vehicle to keep it all together.

Lee Bartell, Provincetown, Massachusetts, US

SERVES 4

Preparation: 10 minutes
Cooking: 60 minutes

6-8 onions, finely sliced

4 tbsp butter or olive oil

1 cup / 240 ml red wine

⅛ cup / 30 ml balsamic vinegar

1 tsp sugar or honey

2 cups / 225 g capellini pasta *

2 cups / 250 g feta cheese

2 tbsp parsley, chopped

 * You could use vermicelli, which is a bit thicker, if you cannot obtain capellini.

1 Put the butter or olive oil into a big pot, add the onions, cover, and cook on a gentle heat, stirring frequently, for 30 minutes until the onions are soft.

2 Now pour in the red wine and continue to cook for about 10 minutes, stirring now and again, to reduce the liquid.

3 At this point, add the balsamic vinegar, sugar or honey. Simmer, uncovered, for a further 10 minutes or so while you cook the pasta according to the instructions.

4 When the pasta is ready, toss with the onions, and sprinkle crumbled feta and parsley on top.

Baked sweet potato casserole

Most sweet potato recipes are made with maple syrup and/or brown sugar. This is much too sweet for us. I found this recipe somewhere and it has been a hit in our family. The natural sweetness of the yam or sweet potato is just perfect. This makes a very healthy, low fat and satisfying meal. We serve it with tossed salad and homemade dressing.

Henriette Faber, Kelowna, British Columbia, Canada

SERVES 4

Preparation: 10 minutes
Cooking: 45 minutes

2 yams or sweet potatoes, thinly sliced

1 onion, sliced finely

3 potatoes, thinly sliced

2 tbsp flour

1 cup / 240 ml bouillon/ stock

2 tbsp dry breadcrumbs

2 tbsp grated cheese

1 tbsp fresh parsley, chopped

oil

salt and pepper

Heat oven to 350°F/180°C/Gas 4

1 Grease a 9-inch x 13-inch/23-cm x 33-cm baking dish.

2 Layer the vegetables with sweet potatoes, then onion, followed by potatoes. Repeat the layers until all is used up.

3 Put the flour in a bowl and gradually pour in the stock, stirring to make a smooth mixture. Season as necessary, and then pour this over the potatoes.

4 Now sprinkle the breadcrumbs on top. Cover and bake for 30 minutes, or until the potatoes are soft.

5 Remove the cover and grate the cheese on top, scatter on the parsley and cook, uncovered, for a further 10 minutes to melt the cheese before serving.

Bibimbap
– vegetables and rice

The South Korean city of Jeonju is associated with *bibimbap*, one of the best-known Korean foods. *Bibimbap* literally means 'mixed rice' – *bibida* means to mix and *pap* is rice in Korean. The vegetarian version makes for a hearty meal. A selection of vegetables (bean sprouts, salad leaves, mushrooms, zucchini/courgette) is served in a large bowl with either a fried or partly raw egg (which may bind the mixture together and is far more appetizing than you might expect, though vegans can leave it out). Rice may either be in the bowl or served separately. The whole lot should be mixed together and eaten with a spoon (which Koreans often opt for where China or Japan would make do with chopsticks).

Deolseot-bibimbap* is exactly the same as *bibimbap*, except that it is served in a sizzling pot – changing the texture of the rice and making the dish even more appetizing.

Jacob Lotinga, Gwangju, South Korea

Jacob Lotinga

Preparation: 30 minutes
Cooking: 40 minutes

1 cucumber, finely sliced into long strips

2 tbsp white vinegar

1 tsp brown sugar

2 cups / 450 g rice

1 egg, beaten +*

2 carrots, cut into thin sticks/ julienned

1 zucchini/courgette, sliced into thin strips

4 mushrooms, sliced finely

5 cups / 375 g spinach or other greens, chopped, parboiled and squeezed to remove excess water

1 cup / 100 g bean sprouts, parboiled and squeezed to remove excess water

2 tbsp sesame oil

1-2 tsp sesame seeds

salt

+ optional
* You can fry the egg and serve it on top, as suggested in the introduction – or make an omelet as described in #3 below.

1 Mix the vinegar with the sugar and soak the cucumber strips in this, turning from time to time while you prepare the rest of the dish.

2 Cook the rice in boiling water for 10-15 minutes.

3 If using the egg for an omelet, heat a little oil in a wok and when hot, pour in the egg, swirling it round the pan to spread out and make an omelet. Cook till browned, and then set aside and cut into strips.

4 Next, sauté the carrots until softening. Then add the zucchini/courgettes and mushrooms. When almost done, add the spinach/greens and bean sprouts and cook for a short while only.

5 Spoon in the sesame oil, half the sesame seeds and a little salt. Stir-fry for a further minute or two.

6 Scoop out onto a serving dish. Add the omelet strips if using, and top with the cucumber and a few more sesame seeds.

Black-eyed beans with okra

Here is a favorite recipe. The first time I had black-eyed beans cooked with vegetables was when I was seven or eight years old. Growing up in Mumbai in the late 1950s-early 1960s I had great fortune and pleasure in being surrounded by different communities from all over India and beyond. Cheek-by-jowl intercultural living was brilliant for learning about different traditions, languages, dress codes and, of course, food. Being a foodie from childhood, I loved the Mumbai custom of neighbors sending each other 'their dish of the day'. Our Sindhi neighbor, Sheila, knew we loved this dish and therefore used to bring over a bowlful every time she cooked it. Needless to say, my mother would always send over dishes that Sheila or her family liked.

The black-eyed beans and okra or *bhindi* can be replaced with any other available bean and vegetable. It is absolutely delicious with rice and goes equally well with flat Indian bread.

Mridu Thanki

SERVES 4

Preparation: 20 minutes
Cooking: 20 minutes

2 potatoes, diced, parboiled and drained

16-20 okra, topped and tailed

2 cans black-eyed beans, drained

2 tbsp cilantro/coriander, chopped

oil *

salt

* Best to use peanut or safflower oil for hot frying.

For baghaar/'tempering':

3 tbsp ghee/ butter

½ tsp cumin seeds

1 onion, finely chopped

1 tbsp fresh ginger, finely chopped

2 cloves garlic, finely chopped

1 tbsp ground coriander

½ tsp turmeric

¼ tsp chili powder

2 tomatoes, chopped

1 Deep-fry, or fry, the potatoes in medium hot oil. Next, fry the okra in very hot oil until just soft and put them aside.

2 Put the beans in a pan, add a little water and bring to a simmer. Heat through thoroughly and then set aside.

3 For the *baghaar*, heat the ghee/butter in a pan. Then add the cumin seeds, and as soon as these brown, put in the onion. Fry that until golden, and then add the ginger and garlic. Cook for a few minutes and then put in the coriander, turmeric and chili powder; stir for few seconds.

4 Next, add the tomatoes, stir, and cook for 5 minutes.

5 Spoon this mixture into the cooked beans. Add the potatoes, bring to the boil and simmer for 5-7 minutes.

6 Finally, gently mix in the okra and seasoning, and cook for another minute until it is heated. Scatter the fresh cilantro/coriander on top before serving.

Bobotie

This is a traditional South African recipe, adapted from its meat-based origins. The name of this popular South African dish probably comes from the Indonesian word *bobotek*. It is likely that the recipe traveled from the Dutch East Indies (now Indonesia).

It has a varied heritage: the Dutch brought ground meat to the local cuisine, the spices were introduced by the slaves from Indonesia and the presentation is reminiscent of English shepherd's pie. But, in my experience, it's more eaten at home than served in restaurants – which is a pity.

SERVES 4

Preparation: 30 minutes
Cooking: 60 minutes

3 or 4 slices bread

1 cup / 240 ml milk

2 onions, chopped

2 cloves garlic, crushed

1-inch/2.5-cm piece
 fresh ginger, grated

¼-½ green chili,
 de-seeded and
 chopped finely

2 tsp garam masala

1 tsp ground cumin

1 tsp ground coriander

4 cloves

8 allspice berries

stick of cinnamon

¾ cup / 100 g dried
 apricots, chopped

2 tbsp sultanas or raisins

1 apple chopped

1 cup / 200 g red lentils,
 washed

2 cups water

1 can rosecoco or black-
 eyed beans, drained

1 egg

3 tbsp parsley, chopped

3 bay leaves

oil, butter or margarine

salt

Topping:

1 tsp turmeric

½ tsp cinnamon powder

1 egg

1 cup / 240 ml milk
 (including retained
 milk from soaked
 bread)

Heat oven to 400°F/200°C/Gas 6

1 First, soak the bread in the milk for about 20-30 minutes, until the milk is fully absorbed and the bread is really soft. When ready, with clean hand, squeeze the bread to release some of the milk (retain this milk).

2 While the bread is soaking, heat the fat in a saucepan and then cook the onions until soft. Next, put in the garlic, ginger, chili, garam masala,

ground cumin, ground coriander, cloves, allspice and cinnamon stick and stir; fry for a couple of minutes.

3 Add water, apricots and sultanas or raisins, apple and lentils and cook for some 20 minutes until the lentils are soft. Leave to cool a little.

4 While cooking, mix the soaked bread with the egg, parsley, bay leaves and the beans. Add this to the lentil mix and squash with your clean hand

so the beans are partly, but not fully, mashed. This should make a moist but not watery mix.

5 Put into a baking dish and smooth the top with a spoon.

6 Now, for the topping, mix the egg, with the retained milk from the soaked bread, adding more milk as necessary to make about 1 cup/240 ml. Mix in the turmeric, cinnamon and salt; stir well. Pour this topping over the bean and lentil mix and put it in the oven.

7 Bake for 40-50 minutes or until the topping has set and is golden brown. Serve with yellow rice with raisins (easy to make by adding a little turmeric while cooking), and 'sambals' such as diced cucumber and yogurt (*raita*), dried coconut, chutneys or apricot jam, sliced tomatoes in a little vinegar with chopped chives or spring onions on top, chopped parsley, and sliced bananas.

Boston baked beans

Boston is also known as 'Beantown', and the association comes from a long tradition of slow-baked beans with molasses/black treacle. This dish probably originated in colonial times when Boston's role producing rum in the 'triangular trade' of slaves, sugar and rum was prominent. Sugar cane came from slave plantations in the West Indies and was made into rum in Boston. Then this was exported and sold to produce money to purchase more slaves. The classic dish uses pork, but this vegetarian version is good and tasty.

SERVES 4 - 6

Preparation: 10 minutes
Cooking: 30 minutes

1 onion, sliced

4 cloves garlic, sliced

1-2 tbsp brown sugar

1 tsp mustard powder

1 tbsp malt vinegar

1 tbsp black treacle/molasses

2 tbsp tomato ketchup

2 cans haricot, navy or cannellini beans, drained (retain liquid)

3-4 cloves

2 bay leaves

½ tsp ground ginger or 1-inch/2.5-cm piece fresh ginger, chopped

1 tsp thyme

1 tsp ground cumin

½ tsp chili powder or cayenne

oil

salt and pepper

1 Pour the oil into a large pan and, when hot, sauté the onion until soft. Then reduce the heat and put in the garlic.

2 In a bowl, mix the ketchup with half the retained bean liquid, 1 tablespoon of the sugar, mustard, vinegar and treacle.

3 Place the beans in the pan with the onions and garlic, and pour in the ketchup mixture. Add the cloves, bay leaves, ginger, thyme, cumin and chili or cayenne; stir well. Add more sugar as desired.

4 Cover the pan and cook at a gentle simmer for 15-20 minutes until the tastes have combined. Add more of the retained bean liquid if the mixture looks too dry.

5 Flavor with salt and pepper, and then serve with baked potatoes or rice and a green salad.

Burritos

A great vegetarian version of the Mexican dish. You can experiment with using other beans, but red kidney beans are the best. Depending on your preference, you can use some of the liquid the kidney beans are in, or add water or stock as required.

SERVES 4

Preparation: 10 minutes
Cooking: 20 minutes

1 onion, sliced

2 cloves garlic, chopped

2 cans red kidney beans

1 can tomatoes, drained (retain liquid)

1 tsp chili powder or ½ tsp chili,
  de-seeded and chopped

1 tsp ground cumin

1 tsp oregano

1 tbsp parsley, chopped

8 tortillas

oil

salt and pepper

UN / F KEERY

1 Using a saucepan, sauté the onion and when it is transparent, add the garlic.

2 Now put in the beans, tomatoes, chili, cumin, oregano and parsley. Add some liquid if required.

3 Bring to a gentle simmer and cook until all the flavors have integrated. Mash the beans; the mixture should not be too sloppy. Season.

4 Place an eighth of the mixture to one side of a tortilla along with salad, sour cream, guacamole, salsa or other ingredients to taste – don't overfill! Fold in each side of the tortilla and then roll to form the burrito.

Butternut squash curry

Butternut squash is a firm favorite. It even looks lovely just sitting in the basket with the other veg – never mind when you cook it, with its delicate orange color and gentle flavor. In this recipe, based on one of Jamie Oliver's, the sweet potatoes and chili make it special and it's a guaranteed crowd-pleaser when friends come to dinner. You can make it even more quickly if you first parboil the butternut and sweet potato in boiling water for 5 minutes or so.

Gabriel Tiranti, Brighton, England

SERVES 4

Preparation: 10 minutes
Cooking: 35 minutes

1 onion, chopped

2 cloves garlic

1-inch/2.5-cm piece fresh lemon grass, chopped

1-inch/2.5-cm piece fresh ginger, peeled and chopped

¼ -½ chili, de-seeded and chopped, or ¼ tsp chili powder

½ tsp turmeric

splash of soy sauce

juice of 1 lime

1 butternut squash, de-seeded and diced

2 sweet potatoes, diced

1 can coconut milk

oil

salt

1 Put the onion, garlic, lemon grass, ginger, chili, turmeric, soy sauce, lime juice, oil and salt in a blender and purée to make a paste.

2 Heat the paste in a pan or wok, stirring, and cook for a couple of minutes before adding the squash and sweet potatoes. Turn them round to coat with the curry flavors.

3 Next, pour in the coconut milk and mix well.

4 Cook gently, uncovered, for 25-30 minutes, until the vegetables are tender and the sauce has thickened. Stir occasionally so that the mixture does not burn. You may need to add a little water from time to time (or more lime juice) to prevent the sauce becoming too dry. Serve with rice or naan bread.

Couscous

A classic Moroccan dish that is cooked in one pot. Ideally, you use a *couscousier* which has a top section with small holes in it. This cooks the couscous grains above the vegetables, so that they imbibe the steamy flavors. But it is fine to cook it separately; see the packet for instructions. You can vary the vegetables and use what you can easily obtain.

SERVES 6-8

Preparation: 15 minutes
Cooking: 30 minutes

2 onions, chopped

2 carrots, sliced finely

1-2 eggplants/
aubergines, diced

2 zucchini/courgettes,
chopped finely

4 cloves garlic, chopped

1-inch/2.5-cm piece fresh
ginger, grated

1 stick cinnamon

2 tsp ground cumin

2 tsp ground coriander

3 cups / 720 ml bouillon/
stock

2 cups / 450 g couscous

1 can garbanzos/
chickpeas, drained

4 tomatoes, chopped

2 tbsp tomato paste/
purée

1 green chili, de-seeded
and chopped or ½ tsp
chili powder

½ tsp saffron strands
soaked in 2 tbsp warm
water for 10 minutes

2 tbsp cilantro/coriander,
chopped

1 tbsp flaked almonds,
toasted *

1 scallion/spring onion,
chopped

1 tbsp margarine

oil

salt

* To toast the flaked almonds,
heat a dry pan and put them
in for a few minutes, stirring
all the time, until they turn
golden brown.

NB If using a *couscousier*, you can cook everything in the bottom section, except the couscous grains, which, after soaking for 10 minutes, go into the top section after #3 below.

1 Heat the oil and sauté the onions for a couple of minutes, followed by the carrots. When they are beginning to sweat, put in the eggplants/aubergines and zucchini/courgettes. Stir for 5 minutes or until they are becoming soft.

2 Next, put in the garlic, ginger, cinnamon, cumin and coriander and stir the mixture gently as it cooks for a few minutes.

3 Gradually pour in the stock, stirring, and then cover the pan and simmer for 10 minutes until everything is cooked through. If using a *couscousier*, put the soaked couscous into the top section and start to cook it above the vegetables at this stage. If not using a

couscousier, carry on with the following instructions and see #6 below.

4 Now put in the garbanzos/chickpeas, tomatoes and tomato paste/purée, chili or chili powder, drained saffron, half of the cilantro/coriander and salt. Stir well.

5 Bring the pan to the boil and stir the contents to cook for a few minutes before turning down to a low heat.

6 If not using a *couscousier*, boil some water and cook the soaked couscous according to the packet instructions.

7 When the couscous in ready, drain it and then stir in the toasted flaked almonds and scallion/spring onion. Pile the couscous on a big flat dish. Heap the vegetables on top of the couscous and garnish with the remaining cilantro/coriander.

Cowpeas/black-eyed beans and pumpkin casserole

Cowpeas (*izindumba*) are commercially grown, available in health shops. They are often known as black-eyed peas or beans. They are an indigenous African legume, and can be used fresh or dried. They are very tasty, high in protein and contain vitamins E, A and C, as well as some selenium, zinc and iron. They grow abundantly in the height of summer when it is difficult to grow popular exotic vegetables like green beans. The leaves can be eaten as spinach.
Mary Kleinenberg, Pietermaritzburg, South Africa

SERVES 4

Preparation: 10 minutes
Cooking: 20 minutes

2 onions, chopped

½ tsp ground cinnamon

2 tsp curry powder

1 tsp paprika

½ tsp mixed spice

pinch of nutmeg

½ tsp thyme

2-3 cloves garlic, sliced

1 pound / 450 g pumpkin or butternut, cut into bite-sized chunks

1 red or green bell pepper, chopped

3 tomatoes, chopped

2 carrots, sliced

1 can black-eyed beans, drained

a little bouillon/stock

salt

Mary Kleinenberg

1 In a lightly oiled pan, fry the onions until they soften, and then add the cinnamon, curry powder, paprika, mixed spice, nutmeg, thyme and garlic and fry for about 5 minutes.

2 Then put in the remaining ingredients, except the beans. Pour in a little stock, cover, bring to the boil and then reduce the heat and cook gently until the pumpkin and carrots are soft, but not breaking up.

3 Turn in the beans, season, and allow to heat through, uncovered. Serve with rice, couscous or quinoa.

vitamins...

Creamy mixed vegetable curry

Growing up in central India, the occasional blander Western-style dish was a welcome change to our usual highly spiced fare. As kids we loved my mum's mixed vegetables in cheesy white sauce. My sister Zarina, who is a wonderful intuitive cook, has developed her own *desi* (twist) on this and surprised me recently with it when I visited her. The recipe below is what I remember of how she cooked it – but has no doubt got 'translated' through the filter of memory. No matter, that's the spirit of Indian cooking – it's supremely adaptable, with each family doing their own version of popular dishes. Both my sister and I use the wholewheat chapati flour called *atta* in this dish – but any flour will do. I've specified *sambar masala*, but if you haven't got any, just use any Indian curry powder. However, if you use garam masala, then leave out the pepper. Feel free to vary the vegetables according to your taste – this is a good way to use up odds and ends. Cheese fiends can add small cubes of cheese towards the end of the cooking.

Dinyar Godrej, Rotterdam, The Netherlands

SERVES 3-4

Preparation: 10 minutes
Cooking: 20 minutes

1-2 tbsp ghee

2 cloves garlic, sliced

½ tsp mustard seeds

1 tsp cumin seeds

1 onion, finely chopped

½-1 green chili, de-seeded, finely sliced

1 tomato, chopped finely

2 carrots, halved lengthways and sliced finely into sticks

1 cup / 150 g green beans* cut into bite-size pieces

½ tsp turmeric

1 tsp ground coriander

¼ tsp freshly ground black pepper

1 tsp sambar masala

1 tbsp flour

2 cups / 150 g mushrooms, sliced finely

1 red bell pepper, diced

1 cup / 240 ml milk

¾ cup / 100 g frozen peas

lime wedges to serve

salt

* Long bean, French, runner or haricot beans.

1 Heat the ghee in a frying pan until hot and throw in the garlic, mustard seeds, cumin seeds, onion and chili. Stir rapidly on high heat for a minute, until the garlic is fragrant and the onion begins to soften.

2 Add the tomato and fry a minute longer. Now add the carrots and beans; stir, then moderate the heat. Cook for 3-4 minutes.

3 Stirring all the time, add the powdered spices. When fragrant add the flour, mushrooms and bell pepper and stir, scraping the pan for a further minute or two. Now add the milk, little by little, stirring all the time.

4 Let the mixture simmer for about 8-10 minutes until the vegetables are nearly done, stirring occasionally, and then add the peas and simmer for a further three minutes. Season with salt and add a little more milk if the sauce is too thick. Serve with lime wedges to cut the creaminess of the dish.

Dal bhat
– lentil curry

I am sending this dal recipe which is Nepali in origin
and made with orange or red lentils.
Abby Shuler

SERVES 4

Preparation: 5 minutes
Cooking: 20 minutes

1 onion, sliced

3 dried red chilies, left whole

1 cup / 200 g red lentils

3 cups/ 720 ml bouillon/stock
  or water

2 tsp turmeric

1-inch/2.5-cm piece fresh
  ginger, chopped

2-4 cloves garlic, chopped

oil

salt

1 In a saucepan, heat the oil and
then fry the onion for a few minutes.
Add the chilies and continue to cook
gently until they begin to brown.

2 Put the lentils in and pour on the
liquid, adding the turmeric. Bring to
the boil and then simmer, covered,
for about 10 minutes until the
mixture thickens.

3 Add the ginger and garlic, stir, and
cook for 5 minutes before serving
with rice.

Empanadas

A recipe from Paraguay, although empanadas are found pretty much throughout the region. They are stuffed pastries or turnovers, and can be made with many different ingredients, including hard-boiled egg with cheese and chili powder. You can also try a mix using crushed sweetcorn or red kidney beans.

SERVES 4

Preparation: 10 minutes
Cooking: 30 minutes

1 pound / 450 g frozen shortcrust or flaky pastry, thawed

1 onion, sliced

1 green bell pepper, chopped

2 cloves garlic, sliced

2-3 hard-boiled eggs, chopped

¼ tsp chili powder

¼ tsp ground cumin

1 tbsp parsley, chopped

oil

salt and pepper

Heat oven to 190°C/375°F/Gas 5

1 Sauté the onion in hot oil and, when it is soft, add the bell pepper and then the garlic. Cook for a couple of minutes and then add the eggs, chili, cumin, parsley and seasoning. Mix well.

2 Roll out the pastry, and then cut into rounds using a saucer.

3 Spoon some of the mix onto one side of the dough and fold the other side over, pressing down the edges with a fork. Prick with a fork to let air escape.

4 Place on a baking sheet, and cook for 10-20 minutes until golden brown. Serve hot with chutney or salsa and a salad.

UN / P Johnson

Ethiopian lentils

Meatless dishes are common in Ethiopia, where fasting days are frequent. Often they use *berbere*, a hot spicy paste that you can purchase in specialty stores or online. This one uses a mix of chili powder and ginger. Red onions are best if you have them.

SERVES 4

Preparation: 10 minutes
Cooking: 25 minutes

1 cup / 225 g red lentils

1 onion, chopped

2 cloves garlic, crushed

1 bell pepper chopped

1 tbsp tomato paste/purée

¼-½ tsp chili powder

½ tsp ground ginger

water or bouillon/stock

salt

1 Wash the lentils and put them in a saucepan with the water or stock to cover, and bring to the boil. Simmer for 15 minutes, and remove any froth on top.

2 Now put in the onion, garlic, bell pepper, tomato paste/purée, chili and ginger. Add more liquid as necessary, and continue to cook for a further 10 minutes or until most of the liquid has been absorbed. Season, and serve with chapatis, pita or rice, and yogurt.

ctsnow under a CC License

Ewa – bean stew

A Nigerian dish like this would be cooked all in one pot, using dried, soaked beans – but you may prefer to use canned beans to shorten the cooking process. You can experiment with different herbs and flavorings.

SERVES 4

Preparation: 10 minutes
Cooking: 25 minutes

1 onion, sliced

1 can beans, such as black-eyed beans, drained

4 tomatoes, chopped

1 green bell pepper, chopped finely

2 tbsp tomato paste/purée

½ tsp chili powder

1-inch/2.5-cm piece fresh ginger, chopped

1 tbsp cilantro/coriander, chopped

1 tbsp lime juice

oil

salt and pepper

1 First cook the onions in oil until they are golden.

2 Add the beans, tomatoes, bell pepper, tomato paste/purée, chili powder, ginger, cilantro/coriander and seasoning. Stir well.

3 Bring the pot to the boil and then reduce the heat and let it simmer for 15-20 minutes until the flavors have combined. Add lime juice and stir. Serve with rice, sweetcorn or bread.

shawn-i-am. under a CC License

Fettuccine Alfredo
– pasta with cashew sauce

After busy after-school activities I needed something quick and nutritious for our four hungry teenagers, and this recipe based on a local vegan cookbook is both very quick to make and delicious. I made a double batch to satisfy their appetite.

Henriette Faber, Kelowna, British Columbia, Canada

S E R V E S   4

Preparation: 10 minutes
Cooking: 20 minutes

1 pound / 450 g fettuccine or tagliatelle pasta

Sauce:
½ cup / 75 g cashews
1 tbsp flour
½ onion, sliced
1 clove garlic, sliced
1 tsp oregano
1 tbsp basil, chopped
1¼ cups / 300 ml water
2 tbsp grated cheese [+]

[+] optional

1 Cook the pasta in ample boiling water for about 10 minutes. Drain.

2 In the meantime, put the cashews, flour, onion, garlic and oregano into a blender. Add the water and blend till creamy.

3 Pour the mixture into a saucepan and bring to a slow boil, stirring frequently until thickened. Now put in half the basil and remove from heat. Ladle over the cooked fettuccine.

4 Sprinkle the cheese (if using) and remaining basil over and serve immediately. It's good with steamed broccoli pieces, dressed with a bit of oil and lemon juice or salad.

Frijoles refritos

This re-fried bean dish is often made with red kidney beans and is a classic Mexican dish. I got to like it a lot when I was traveling in Central America, but not everyone takes to it. It's often served with scrambled eggs, so quite nutritious. And the addition of a salad makes a good meal.

SERVES 4

Preparation: 10 minutes
Cooking: 20 minutes

2 onions, sliced

1 can red kidney beans, drained

4 tomatoes, sliced

1 tbsp tomato paste/purée

½ tsp paprika

2 tsp ground cumin

¼ chili, de-seeded and chopped or ½ tsp chili powder

2 tbsp parsley, chopped

grated cheese or scrambled eggs +

oil

salt and pepper

+ optional

1 Heat the oil in a pan and fry the onions. When golden, put in the beans, mashing them with a fork as they cook.

2 Add the tomatoes, tomato paste/purée, paprika, cumin, chopped chilies or chili powder, half the parsley, salt and pepper. Mix well.

3 Transfer the mixture to a shallow flame-proof dish, and grate the cheese on top, if using.

4 Cook under the grill until hot, or the cheese has melted. If having scrambled eggs, make these while the beans are under the grill. Scatter the remaining parsley on top before serving.

UN / Jerry Frank

Gado-gado
– Southeast Asian salad

This salad is popular both in Indonesia and Malaysia. Tofu is high in calcium, iron and B vitamins, but low in fat and sodium, and is a good source of vegetarian protein.

SERVES 2-3

Preparation: 20 minutes
Cooking: 10 minutes

1 cup / 225 g tofu, cubed and fried

1 cup / 100 g cabbage, shredded

1 cup / 150 g French beans, cut into ½-inch/1-cm pieces

1 potato, sliced thinly

1 carrot, cut into thin sticks

2 cups / 200 g bean sprouts

½ cucumber, sliced

2 hard-boiled eggs, quartered +

Sauce:

1 cup / 125 g peanuts

2 shallots, sliced

4 cloves garlic

2 red chilies, de-seeded and sliced, or 1 tsp chili powder

3 tbsp soy sauce

1 tsp brown sugar

2-3 tbsp lemon or lime juice

1-2 cups / 240-480 ml water

oil

salt

+ optional

1 Start by boiling or steaming all the vegetables, except the bean sprouts and cucumber, for a few minutes until they are just cooked but still crunchy. Drain.

2 Arrange the vegetables on a dish and add the bean sprouts and cucumber. Put the fried tofu cubes on.

3 Make the sauce by blending the peanuts with the shallots, garlic and chili or chili powder (add a little oil if necessary).

4 Then transfer this to a pan and add the soy sauce, sugar, lemon or lime juice and salt and stir well. Cook gently for a few minutes, adding water, and adjusting the soy, sugar and lemon or lime juice levels to your taste.

5 Pour the sauce over the vegetables and decorate with the quartered eggs.

Green bean bredie/stew

A South African dish, *bredie* means stew, and commonly these dishes contain meat. But it is easy to adapt them, as with this one using green beans. Normally bredies are served with rice.

SERVES 4

Preparation: 10 minutes
Cooking: 20 minutes

2 onions, chopped

2-4 cloves garlic, chopped

1-inch/2.5-cm piece fresh ginger, chopped

¼ chili, de-seeded and chopped or ½ tsp chili powder

1 tsp thyme

½ tsp ground coriander

3 cups / 450 g green beans, cut into 1-inch/2.5-cm lengths

2 potatoes, diced

4 tomatoes, chopped

water

oil

salt and pepper

1 Fry the onions in the oil until brown. Add the garlic, ginger, chili, thyme and coriander.

2 Cook for a couple of minutes and then add the beans, potatoes and tomatoes, and mix well.

3 Pour on water barely to cover and bring to the boil. Simmer gently, covered. Add the salt and pepper as you stir round. You can partially mash the mix if preferred, before serving with yellow rice – that is, rice cooked with a bit of turmeric or saffron in it.

pashasha under a CC License

Instant khaman dhokla – garbanzo/chickpea patties

This uses chickpea or gram flour (also called *besan* in India) mixed with yogurt and spices to make a thick batter. The batter is then steamed; seasoned with mustard seeds and served with fresh coriander.

This is a Gujarati dish; I use Eno fruit salt which is a mix of baking soda (bicarbonate) and citric acid and a good aid to digestion. It's in most Asian shops, but you could just use a bit of baking soda instead. Remember for the batter that you want a thick mix that goes drip, drip, drip from the spatula rather than a pouring consistency.

Mari Marcel Thekaekara, Tamil Nadu, India

SERVES 4

Preparation: 10 minutes
Cooking: 45 minutes

1 cup / chickpea flour

2 tbsp sugar

1 tbsp oil

1 tbsp lime or lemon juice

½-1 green chili, de-seeded, finely sliced

½ cup / 120 ml water

1 tsp Eno fruit salt or baking soda

salt

For the seasoning:

2 tbsp oil

1 tsp mustard seeds

4-5 curry leaves, crushed

pinch asafetida*

2 tbsp hot water

1 tbsp sugar +

2 tbsp lime or lemon juice

2 tbsp cilantro/coriander, chopped

* Asafetida is a highly aromatic resin, available from specialty or Asian shops.
+ optional

1 Mix together the chickpea flour, salt, sugar, 1 tbsp oil and the same of lime or lemon juice, the chili and add most of the water, stirring to make a thick creamy batter.

2 Take a large pan that can be used as a steamer, or use a pressure cooker, and pour in about 3 cups/720 ml water to heat up. Grease a bowl which can fit snugly in the steamer or pressure cooker; it can be lined with baking paper if you want.

3 Now add the salts or baking soda to the batter and mix well. Spoon the batter into the bowl and place in the pressure cooker or steamer immediately, and steam for 15 minutes or so.

4 Then turn off the heat and leave it to rest for 3 minutes, and test with a toothpick. This should come out clean. When ready, take out the dhokla and cut it into squares.

5 For the seasoning, heat the oil, add the mustard seeds, curry leaves and a pinch of asafetida. When the mustard seeds pop, turn off the flame.

6 Mix together the hot water with the sugar, if using, and lime juice until the sugar dissolves. Pour this into the seasoning. If you prefer to omit the sugar, you can just add hot water to the oil.

7 Pour the seasoning over the dhoklas, scatter on the cilantro/coriander leaves and serve hot.

Irio
– bean and corn mash

This mix of beans and corn is common in parts of East Africa, and uses greens called *sukumu wiki* ('stretch the week' in KiSwahili). You can add a bit of butter or margarine for a richer mixture.

1 onion, chopped

½ tsp paprika

2 tbsp fresh parsley, chopped

1 can beans, such as pinto or black-eyed (keep liquid)

1 can sweetcorn (keep liquid)

4 potatoes, cut into chunks and parboiled

½ pound / 250 g spinach or greens, chopped

oil

salt and pepper

1 Heat the oil and sauté the onion. When soft, sprinkle in the paprika and half of the parsley, and stir.

2 Now put in the beans and sweetcorn with some of their liquid, and the parboiled potatoes. Cover and bring to the boil, stirring from time to time.

3 Add the chopped greens and seasoning. Cook for 5-10 minutes until the potatoes are soft and the ingredients have absorbed the flavors.

4 Remove from the heat and roughly mash the ingredients; decorate with the remaining parsley on top. The dish would normally be served with *ugali*, maize porridge. But it is good with rice or potatoes, and a relish or spicy salsa-type sauce.

Ai@ce under a CC License

Lasagna

Lasagna has a special place in my memory. We were staying with my cousin, Sue, a farmer in Lincolnshire, England. She cooked this for our dinner but while serving she received an emergency call and dashed out to deliver a calf – successfully, I'm glad to say.

If you can, use *puy* green lentils, grown in the Le Puy region of France. They stay firm when cooked and have a good flavor, with plenty of 'mouth feel' – in other words, they add substance to the dish.

SERVES 4 - 6

Preparation: 20 minutes
Cooking: 20 minutes

6-8 lasagna sheets

1¼ cups / 225 g green lentils, soaked

1-2 onions, sliced

2-3 cloves garlic

1 red bell pepper, chopped

1 green bell pepper, chopped

6-10 mushrooms, sliced

2 cans tomatoes

2-4 tbsp tomato paste/purée

2 tsp dried oregano

½ tsp paprika

pinch of nutmeg

oil

salt and pepper

Sauce:

2 tbsp butter or margarine

2-3 tbsp plain flour

1¼ cups / 300 ml milk

2 cups / 200 g cheese, grated

1 tbsp parsley, chopped

salt and pepper

Heat oven to 350°F/180°C/Gas 4

1 Cook the lentils in stock or water for about 15 minutes until they are tender; drain and rinse.

2 Using a large pan, fry the onions and garlic until soft. Then add more oil if/ as necessary and sauté the bell peppers; stir-fry for a few minutes. Follow them with the mushrooms, cook to soften a

little before spooning in the lentils. Stir to mix the ingredients.

3 Next, add the canned tomatoes and tomato paste/purée, the oregano, paprika, nutmeg and seasoning. Leave to simmer gently while you make the sauce.

4 For the sauce, melt the butter or margarine in a pan then add the flour, stirring well to make a smooth mix.

Cook for half a minute or so and then very slowly add the milk, stirring all the time so that the sauce is smooth, without lumps. Continue to cook for 5 minutes or so, stirring, until the sauce thickens. ﹨

5 Place half the lasagna sheets on the bottom of the dish, and spoon the vegetable mixture over.

6 Next, cover this with lasagna sheets and remaining sauce. Now pour on the white sauce; smooth over the top. Grate the cheese over.

7 Place the lasagna in the preheated oven for about 20 minutes until it is browned on top. Sprinkle the parsley on top and serve.

Moussaka

I think the first time I tasted this was when I traveled to Istanbul in the early 1970s, as a short break from setting up the *New Internationalist* magazine. I'd never really encountered this type of Middle Eastern food before. It was in some small eatery, and the experience was made all the more fascinating by the cook's insistence that we come into the kitchen to sample all the dishes first. What a good idea!

The Turks spell the dish *musakka*: the word derives from the Arabic for 'chilled'.

<u>S E R V E S   4 - 6</u>

Preparation: 20 minutes
Cooking: 60 minutes

2 onions, chopped

2 cups / 200 g mushrooms, sliced

2 tbsp tomato paste/purée

1 can tomatoes

4 cloves garlic, crushed

1 bay leaf

1 tsp oregano

½ tsp or 1 stick cinnamon

6 potatoes, parboiled and cut into ¼-inch/1-cm slices and parboiled

2 eggplants/aubergines, cut into very thin slices

Sauce:

2 tbsp butter or margarine

3 tbsp flour

2 cups / 480 ml milk

1 cup / 100 g grated cheese

1 tbsp parsley, chopped

oil

salt and pepper

Heat oven to 350°F/180°C/Gas 4

1 Heat the oil in a large pan and sauté the onions. Add the mushrooms and tomato paste/purée and cook for 5 minutes.

2 Now put in the tomatoes, garlic, bay leaf, oregano, cinnamon, salt and pepper. Cover, and cook for 10 minutes over a gentle heat. Add a little water if the mix is very dry.

3 After this, place a layer of potato slices over the base of a rectangular baking dish. Then cover with a layer of eggplant/ aubergine, and top that with the mushroom and tomato mix. Repeat until all the ingredients are used up.

4 Next, make the white sauce by melting the margarine or butter in a heavy saucepan over medium heat. Slowly shake in the flour, stirring constantly to make a smooth mixture. Then gradually pour in the milk, again stirring all the time so that the sauce is smooth. Cook for 3 minutes or until the sauce thickens.

5 Spoon the sauce on top of the moussaka. Then cover the dish and bake for approx. 30 minutes until cooked.

6 Remove the lid and sprinkle the cheese over. Brown for 5-10 minutes and then scatter the parsley on top before serving.

Mushroom stroganoff

I was keen to try this stroganoff recipe, a version of Mr Oliver's. Classically made with beef, the substitution of chestnut mushrooms makes for a tasty dish (and ordinary mushrooms are also ok). And if you're feeling naughty, use cream or crème fraîche...
Gabriel Tiranti, Brighton, England

SERVES 4

Preparation: 15 minutes
Cooking: 20 minutes

1 onion, sliced finely

4 cloves garlic, crushed

1 pound / 450 g mushrooms, chopped

1 tsp paprika

pinch of nutmeg

½ cup / 120 ml white wine

1 tbsp balsamic vinegar

2 tbsp cilantro/coriander, chopped

3 tbsp yogurt, cream or crème fraîche

water

oil

salt and pepper

1 Heat the oil in a large pan and then sauté the onion for a few minutes before adding the garlic.

2 Now turn up the heat and put in the mushrooms. Sprinkle the paprika and nutmeg over them and stir so that they are coated. Cook for about 10 minutes until the mushrooms are soft and brown.

3 Next, pour in the wine and balsamic vinegar; stir. Reduce the heat and then simmer gently.

4 Put in the cilantro/coriander and yogurt, cream or crème fraîche. Season, mix well and serve with mashed potato or rice and salad.

Nasi goreng

A popular dish in Indonesia and Malaysia – and one that I often enjoyed when I lived for a year in Penang. Nasi goreng (fried rice) features in both Malaysian and Indonesian cuisine. It has an interesting blend of tastes and textures. In the Far East the dish generally includes a dried shrimp paste called *blachan* in Malaysia and *terasi* in Indonesia, but this recipe substitutes bean curd/tofu. Some recipes have an omelet added. This is cooked first and then cut into strips and added to the dish at the end.

<u>SERVES 4 - 6</u>

Preparation: 20 minutes
Cooking: 15 minutes

2 cups / 450 g rice

2 eggs, beaten

3 shallots, sliced

2 scallions/spring onions, sliced finely

½-inch/1-cm fresh ginger, chopped or 1 tsp powdered ginger

1 carrot, sliced into thin sticks

1 cup / 100 g white cabbage, sliced finely

1 tbsp sultanas

1 cup / 225 g bean curd/tofu, diced

1 tbsp curry paste or chili sauce

1 tbsp soy sauce

1 tsp sesame oil

½ cucumber, sliced

2 tbsp cilantro/coriander, chopped

oil

salt

1 Cook the rice in boiling water for 10-15 minutes, and then drain.

2 While the rice is cooking, season the beaten eggs. Heat some oil in a frying pan and when hot, pour in the eggs and swirl round to make an omelet. Cook for a few minutes until golden, and then tip it out onto a plate. Roll it up, leave to cool and then slice into strips.

3 Now heat some more oil and sauté the shallots, scallions/spring onions and ginger for a minute or two. Then add the carrot, cabbage and sultanas and continue to stir-fry for 3 minutes until tender.

4 Next, put in the cooked rice and bean curd/tofu and toss with the vegetables. Combine the soy sauce, sesame oil and curry paste/chili sauce. Pour this over the ingredients and mix well. Adjust the flavorings to taste.

5 Arrange the omelet strips and cucumber slices on top and scatter the cilantro/coriander over before serving.

Orange vegetable bake

This is a good dish for vegan friends as it is really nice served with couscous for a main course. Toasted almonds or pine nuts add a bit of protein and crunch. It can also be served as a side dish with a roast or curry. Select any orange veg you have – carrots, butternut squash, sweet potato, pumpkin, bell pepper – you can use one or all. It is very easy to make and can be varied with other seasonal veg if you prefer, such as new potatoes. I use whole garlic – young garlic from the garden is hard to beat.
Helen Beinart, Oxford, England

<u>SERVES 4</u>

Preparation: 10 minutes
Cooking: 30 minutes

2 pounds / 900 g mixed vegetables, such as carrots, butternut squash, sweet potato, pumpkin, bell pepper, chopped or sliced finely

1 head of garlic, unpeeled

½ tsp ground cumin

½ tsp ground coriander

oil

salt and pepper

Heat to 425°F/220°C/Gas 7

1 Put the vegetables in a large bowl and toss in some olive oil, with the herbs and seasoning.

2 Add the garlic head – you can separate the cloves if you prefer, but don't peel them.

3 Now lay the vegetables flat in a baking dish and roast for about 30 minutes or until soft. Keep an eye on them and stir from time to time to prevent catching.

Pasta with broccoli, sundried tomato and feta

This dish was inspired by a similar one seen on an Irish cooking show many years ago. Something about the combination of ingredients just works in a beautiful and satisfying taste, texture and nutritional harmony; it's also dead simple and quick to make. I might add that it's almost impossible to get wrong, unless you overcook the broccoli. It's the sort of dish that's a great stay-at-home comfort food meal, and equally impressive in any company. Eat! Enjoy! And only two pots to wash!

Aadhaar O'Gorman, Bunbury, Western Australia

SERVES 4-6

Preparation: 10 minutes
Cooking: 25 minutes

1 onion, chopped

1 cup / 150 g sundried tomatoes, soaked, and sliced into strips

1 pound / 450 g pasta *

1 head broccoli, cut into florets

½ tsp ground cumin

1 tsp dried or 2 tbsp fresh basil, chopped

2 tbsp pine nuts

1½ cups / 150 g feta cheese, cubed

oil

salt and pepper

* Any pasta will do, but try fusilli, spirali or soyaroni.

1 Put on a large pot of water for the pasta – make it extra big, because the broccoli's going in here too.

2 Heat the oil and fry the onion. As it becomes translucent add the sundried tomatoes. Be gentle with the cooking, this dish doesn't need much.

3 Pop the pasta into the boiling water, and when you're about 5 minutes from its being ready, throw in the broccoli florets.

4 Back to the pan, add the cumin, the basil (if you're using dried) and the pine nuts. A low heat is enough to see this through while the broccoli and pasta are finishing up.

5 If you're using fresh basil, chop it up well and add it only about a minute before it all comes together.

6 When the pasta and broccoli are done and drained, combine the lot (toss it all together), season to taste, and add the feta. Stir to mix, and serve.

Phad Thai

A signature dish of Thailand, normally containing prawns and sometimes also pork. The noodles are rice noodles if you can find them, but fettuccine will do instead.

SERVES 4

Preparation: 20 minutes
Cooking: 20 minutes

1 pound / 450 g flat noodles

1 pack firm bean curd/tofu, diced

½ cup / 80 g peanuts, chopped/crushed

2 eggs, beaten [+]

1 onion, sliced

2 cloves, garlic, crushed

½ green chili, de-seeded and chopped

¼ tsp ginger or 1-inch/2.5-cm piece fresh ginger, crushed

1 red bell pepper, sliced finely

¼ cup / 60 g peanut butter

4-6 scallions/spring onions, sliced

1-2 tbsp cilantro/coriander, chopped

1 cup / 100 g bean sprouts

¼ cup / 60 ml soy sauce

juice of 1-2 limes

1 tbsp brown sugar

peanut oil

[+] optional

1 Bring some water to boil and add the noodles; cook for 5-10 minutes until soft. Drain.

2 While that is happening, fry the diced tofu in the wok or pan until golden; set aside. Then toast the chopped or crushed peanuts in a little oil until they just start to brown.

3 If using the eggs, heat some oil in the pan and, when hot, pour in the eggs and make a light omelet. Cook for a few minutes until it sets and then remove and set aside. Cut into thin strips.

4 Next, sauté the onion, garlic, chili, ginger and bell pepper. Stir-fry for 2-3

minutes. When the onion is soft, put in the peanut butter and mix well. Then add the noodles and stir them in.

5 Next, add the cooked bean curd/ tofu, scallions/spring onion, bean sprouts, omelet strips and half the cilantro/coriander. Heat through, stirring.

6 In a bowl, mix together the soy sauce, lime juice and sugar. Pour over the noodles and stir to blend in the sauce. Scatter the peanuts and remaining cilantro/coriander on top before serving.

Picadillo

There are many ways to make this Latin American dish with some variation on the ingredients below. It has a lovely complex flavor and the mix also makes a great filling for burritos (p 76) or empanadas (p 88).

Achiote oil uses annatto (bixa) seeds which give color and flavor. You could use ordinary oil instead and add ½ tsp of turmeric.

<u>SERVES 2-4</u>

Preparation: 15 minutes
Cooking: 25 minutes

1-2 onions, chopped

1-2 green or red bell peppers, chopped

2 cloves garlic, crushed

½ tsp cayenne pepper

¼-½ tsp turmeric *

1 can black beans, drained

4 tomatoes, chopped or 1 can tomatoes

1 tbsp sultanas or raisins

2 tbsp capers

1-2 tsp ground cumin

1 tsp oregano

½ tsp thyme

12 green olives

¼ cup / 60 ml achiote oil *

salt and pepper

* To make achiote oil, heat ½ cup/50 g annatto seeds in 1 cup/240 ml vegetable oil. Boil until oil is deep bright orange. Strain seeds from oil. Instead of this you can use ordinary vegetable oil and add ½ tsp turmeric, to give the color.

1 Heat the oil in a large pan. Put in the onions and cook until soft. Then add the bell peppers, garlic and cayenne, plus the turmeric if using. Fry gently for a few minutes to soften the peppers.

2 Next, add the beans, tomatoes, sultanas or raisins, capers, cumin, oregano and thyme. Season, and stir.

3 Reduce the heat now and leave to simmer for 10-15 minutes to deepen the flavors. Now put in the olives and simmer for a few more minutes to warm them through. Serve with potatoes or rice.

Pipérade

Pipérade is a specialty from the Basque region of southern France and northern Spain. It's the way to use the seasonal glut of tomatoes and peppers in the region, and delivers bright summery colors and tastes.

SERVES 4

Preparation: 5 minutes
Cooking: 15 minutes

1 onion, finely sliced

2 red bell peppers, chopped

3-4 tomatoes, chopped

2 cloves garlic, chopped

¼ tsp paprika

1 bay leaf

½ tsp thyme

4 eggs, beaten

oil

salt and pepper

1 Heat some olive oil in a large frying pan. Gently cook the onion until it is soft.

2 Add the bell peppers, and cook gently for 10 minutes.

3 Now add the tomatoes, garlic, paprika, bay leaf and thyme, and continue to cook until the mixture has blended. Season.

4 Turn up the heat and add the beaten eggs to the pan. Cook, stirring to mix the ingredients. Remove from the heat when the eggs start to thicken and serve at once, with crusty bread.

Porotos con mazamorra – bean and pumpkin dish

Porotos means beans in South America. This dish from Chile is a variant of many similar dishes in the region using the local staples beans, pumpkin and sweetcorn.

<u>SERVES 4-6</u>

Preparation: 15 minutes
Cooking: 20 minutes

1 onion, chopped

2 cloves garlic, chopped

4 tomatoes, chopped

1 tsp paprika

½ cumin seeds

1 can flageolet or white kidney beans

1 can sweetcorn, drained

2 cups / 250 g pumpkin, cut into small chunks and parboiled

2 tbsp basil, chopped

a little water/milk mix

oil

salt and pepper

1 Sauté the onion in a pan and when it is soft, add the garlic and the tomatoes, paprika and cumin seeds. Cook for a further minute or so.

2 Next, put the beans and the sweetcorn into the pan. When these are warmed through, add the parboiled pumpkin pieces and a little water/milk mix. Stir well.

3 Cook for 5 minutes or until everything is soft. Then lightly mash the ingredients together with the back of a wooden spoon or a potato masher. Season, and add half the basil; stir. Add more liquid as required to get the consistency you prefer.

4 Cook over a low heat and, when hot, scatter the basil on top. Serve with mashed or baked potatoes.

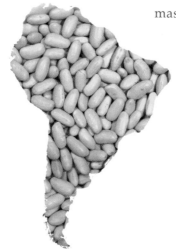

Quick and easy nut loaf

As vegetarians for most of our lives, and living in a cold country like England, we've always found it important to have a nut roast for a warming family Sunday dinner to go alongside potatoes and fresh vegetables. We've tried many different recipes over the years but none has suited us as well as this one, which was handed on to us through the family. It is amazingly quick and simple to concoct but also fantastically flavorsome. We'd normally serve it with a tasty gravy and cranberry sauce.
Chris Brazier and Pat Tope, Oxford, England

SERVES 3-4

Preparation: 5 minutes
Cooking; 35 minutes

1 onion, chopped coarsely

1½ cups / 225 g mixed nuts *

2 cups / 200 g wholemeal bread

1½ cups / 300 ml bouillon/stock

2 eggs

2 tsp mixed herbs

salt and pepper

* Brazil nuts are especially good, but hazelnuts and walnuts are fine, alongside the peanuts/groundnuts that keep the cost down.

Heat oven to 350°C/180°C/Gas 4

1 The easiest thing is to bung all the ingredients above into a food-processor – even the onion does not need pre-cooking.

2 Then simply pour the mixture into a suitable dish (flame-proof glass is as good as a metal loaf tin) and bake for 35 minutes.

Ratatouille

Ratatouille originated in the area around what is now Provence in France. Versions of the dish are found in Catalunya and Majorca. An exuberant dish, it's good to make lots and freeze some for when summer is over to remind you of sunny days. Serve with hot bread.

SERVES 4-6

Preparation: 15 minutes
Cooking: 2-4 hours

2 onions, chopped finely

3 cloves garlic, chopped

1 can tomatoes

1 eggplant/aubergine, diced

2 sticks celery, chopped finely

2 zucchini/courgettes, sliced

1 green bell pepper, chopped finely

1 red bell pepper, chopped finely

1-2 tbsp tomato paste/purée

2 tsp sugar

2 tbsp parsley, chopped

1 tsp oregano, or ½ tsp dried

1-2 tbsp fresh basil, chopped

oil

salt and pepper

Heat oven to 250°F/130°C/Gas ½-1

1 Using a heavy pan that can also go into the oven, put a little oil in and then sauté the onions, followed by the garlic.

2 Then put in the remaining ingredients and seasoning; stir well.

3 Cover the pan and then cook very gently in the oven for 2-4 hours until everything is combined and rich. You can serve it hot or warm, with crusty bread.

Salade Niçoise

A classic French salad dish, with many versions. I have fond memories of it, as almost the first meal I ever ate in Paris, a long time ago. My brother David was working there and I took refuge with him after work/boyfriend disasters in London. For my first lunch, we went to some little place and I had *Salade Niçoise** and *un petit ballon de vin blanc*. Both were delicious; I was hooked on *la vie parisienne*, found a job, and stayed for two years.

* That recipe would have included tuna but the recipe here uses garbanzos/chickpeas instead. If you do use tuna, take care to avoid bluefin tuna, which is now critically endangered.

Preparation: 10 minutes
Cooking: 5 minutes

1-2 potatoes, diced

5-10 green beans, cut into 2-inch/5-cm pieces

1 can garbanzos/chickpeas, drained

1 lettuce

2 tomatoes, cut into quarters

2 eggs, hard-boiled, cut into quarters

1 tbsp green or black olives, pitted

1 tbsp fresh parsley, chopped

Dressing:
lemon juice

olive oil

salt and pepper

1 Boil the diced potatoes and then the beans. Leave to cool.

2 Place the potatoes and beans in a bowl with the garbanzos/chickpeas, lettuce and tomatoes. Mix well.

3 Make up the dressing and toss the salad.

4 Now arrange the egg wedges, olives and parsley on top. Serve with hot, crusty bread.

Speedy cabbage curry

When I left India some 20 years ago and came to England to study, I discovered that cabbage had a pretty poor reputation. I couldn't understand it, as we cooked it in a variety of simple and tasty ways back home and thoroughly enjoyed it. Besides, for a student on a tight budget, its cheapness made it immediately attractive. But when I learnt that many Brits *boiled* this poor vegetable, all became clear…!

This dish is best cooked with the white or the quick-cooking green variety of cabbage as it contrasts the mild bitterness of the cumin and fenugreek with the sweetness of the cabbage. It won't suit the Savoy variety. Keep everything ready before starting this dish as the cooking goes very fast. You can also add peas to this dish if you like, but remember to only just cook them or they will lose their sweetness.

Dinyar Godrej, Rotterdam, The Netherlands

SERVES 4

Preparation: 5 minutes
Cooking: 5-10 minutes

1-inch/2.5-cm piece fresh ginger, cut into narrow strips

1 tsp cumin seeds

½ tsp fenugreek seeds

½ tsp turmeric

1 tsp ground coriander

1 tsp curry powder

1 cup / 240 ml coconut milk

1 cabbage*, cut into four lengthwise and then into thin strips across

2 tbsp cilantro/coriander, chopped

oil

salt

lime juice

* Not savoy cabbage

1 Heat up some oil in a wok or similar pan and throw in the ginger, cumin and fenugreek. Stir rapidly for half a minute and then add the turmeric, coriander and curry powder, give a quick stir and spoon in the coconut milk.

2 Stirring, bring it up to a brisk simmer and add the cabbage. Now turn up the heat and cook, again stirring, until the cabbage is still crunchy and just done – a matter of minutes.

3 Add salt, lime juice to taste and sprinkle with the cilantro/coriander to serve. This goes well with plain boiled rice.

Soybean bake

Friends from the US served us this while we were living and working in Canada for a year and, slightly adapted from a Moosewood original, it has been a regular staple for us ever since – though we've never encountered anyone in Britain who knows it. The preparation may sound daunting given that the soy beans are best soaked overnight but actually that is the only element that requires forethought, as if they are adequately soaked the beans do not need pre-cooking.

Following the instructions in the recipe will certainly lead to a better result but we sometimes save time by adding everything, bar the chopped tomatoes and the green pepper (including the raw onion), to the food-processor once the soybeans have been ground into a batter. Good with salsa (see p 200).

Chris Brazier and Pat Tope, Oxford, England

Preparation: 20 minutes
Cooking: 60 minutes

¾ cup / 150 g soybeans, soaked overnight

1 cup / 225 g bulgur

1 cup / 240 ml boiling water

1 onion, finely chopped

3-4 cloves garlic, crushed

2 tsp ground cumin

2-3 tsp dried basil

½ tsp paprika

1 green or red bell pepper, diced

1 can chopped tomatoes, drained

3 tbsp tomato paste/purée

1 tbsp sultanas [+]

2 tbsp parsley, chopped

2 cups / 250 g feta cheese, crumbled

oil

salt and pepper

[+] optional

Heat oven to 375°F/190°C/Gas 5

1 Lightly oil a 9-inch x 13-inch/23-cm x 33-cm baking tin.

2 Using a small bowl, put in the bulgur and pour on the boiling water. Cover with a plate and leave it to stand for 15 minutes.

3 While that is happening, heat the oil in a large frying pan. Add the onion, garlic, cumin, basil and seasoning. Stir

as you sauté for 5 minutes or so. Then put in the bell pepper and fry gently for a further 5 minutes.

4 Drain the soaked soybeans and spoon them into a food-processor with 1 cup water. Process until the soybeans are like a coarse batter. Transfer this to a large bowl.

5 Add the soaked bulgur and sautéed vegetables to the soybean batter. Stir in

the tomatoes, and then add the tomato paste/purée, sultanas if using, parsley and 1 cup of feta. Mix well.

6 Spoon into the baking tin and scatter the remaining feta on top. Cover, and bake for 30 minutes; then reduce the heat to 350°F/180°C/Gas 4 and continue to cook for 15 minutes before serving.

Sweet potato and cheese patties

I have long been interested in indigenous vegetables and their nutritional properties; I prefer the term 'traditional' because of the tenuousness of the dividing line between vegetables from other parts of the world which have long been consumed in Africa. The sweet potato was introduced from America, and has become very popular in southern Africa. It offers a good source of minerals, vitamins and fiber. Sweet potatoes are a good choice for diabetics because they are at the lower end of the Glycaemic Index, which means that they take a longer time than ordinary potatoes to convert to blood sugar.

Young fresh sweet potato leaves (*Amakhasi kabhatata*) contain iron, zinc, selenium, vitamins C, A and E, carotenoids and protein and make tasty substitutes for other leafy green vegetables.

Mary Kleinenberg, Pietermaritzburg, South Africa

<u>S E R V E S   4 - 6</u>

Preparation: 5 minutes
Cooking: 10 minutes

4 sweet potatoes, chopped

1½ cups / 150 g cheese, diced

2 tbsp roasted* sesame seeds/ sunflower seeds, or a mix

¼ tsp chili powder, or to taste

salt and pepper

* Using a heavy pan with no oil, toast the seeds until they turn golden, stirring frequently.

1 Cook the sweet potatoes in boiling water until soft; drain well. Then mash the potatoes and add the feta cheese, as much chili as you like, and season to taste.

2 Form the mixture into patties or balls, and then roll them in the roasted sesame or sunflower seeds. They are delicious served cold with baby beetroot.

'Swooning Imam' – eggplant/aubergine bake

This recipe from Turkey has to go in the book on the strength of its name alone! There are as many theories as to why the imam fainted as there are recipes for this tasty dish. One is that the imam was overcome when he tasted how delicious it was... In addition to the side sauce below, serve with rice or bread.

Andrew Hine, London, England

<u>SERVES 4</u>

Preparation: 15 minutes
Cooking: 65 minutes

2 onions, sliced

1 red bell pepper, diced

1 green bell pepper, diced

3-4 cloves garlic, crushed

¼ tsp ground cumin

¼ tsp ground coriander

6 tomatoes, chopped finely

2 tbsp parsley, chopped

3 eggplants/aubergines

1 tbsp lemon juice

1 tsp sugar

boiling water

oil

salt and pepper

Side sauce:

1 cup / 240 ml yogurt

1 tbsp mint, chopped finely

Heat oven to 190°C/375°F/Gas 5

1 Heat some oil in a pan and cook the onions till translucent. Then add the bell peppers and cook till they begin to soften.

2 Now put in the garlic, cumin and coriander. Cook slowly until the peppers are soft. Add the tomatoes and parsley; simmer gently.

3 While that is cooking, cut the eggplants/aubergines into halves, leaving the stalks on. Carefully scoop out most of the pulp. Cut this up finely and add to the tomato mixture.

4 Stir well, adding more oil as necessary, and put in the lemon juice and sugar. Simmer for about 20 minutes or until the ingredients are cooked, and then season. The mixture should not be too wet.

5 Wash and dry the eggplant/aubergine shells and place them side by side in an oven-proof dish.

6 Fill the shells with the cooked mixture, and then add enough boiling water to cover the base of the dish, about ¼-inch/½-cm deep. Put a lid or kitchen foil on the dish and bake for 30-45 minutes until the eggplant/ aubergine shells are cooked and the liquid has been absorbed. Remove from the oven and leave to cool to room temperature.

7 In a small bowl, mix the yogurt with the mint.

Vegan nut roast with caramelized onion sauce

SERVES 4

Preparation: 10 minutes
Cooking: 45 minutes

2-3 onions, chopped

4 cloves garlic, crushed

1½ cups / 250 g roasted peanuts

¾ cup / 75 g oats

2 tbsp mixed seeds, such as
   sunflower, pumpkin, linseed,
   sesame

1 can kidney beans, drained

2 cups / 200 g breadcrumbs

2 apples, grated

2 carrots, grated

¼ cup / 60 ml bouillon/stock

2 tsp herbes de provence*

oil

salt and pepper

* Or whatever you have to hand.

For the caramelized onion sauce

2-3 onions, chopped finely

4 cloves garlic, crushed

1 tbsp brown sugar

2-4 mushrooms, finely chopped

6 sundried tomatoes, finely
   chopped

2 tbsp tomato paste/purée

2 tsp stock powder or yeast
   extract or ½ stock cube

dash soy sauce

dash balsamic vinegar

1½ cups / 360 ml water

oil

This is a vego Christmas dinner devised while in Britain, based on something served in cafés I've worked in in Adelaide. It is superb with caramelized onion gravy (see below) and roasted veggies. *Herbes de Provence*, used here, includes basil, fennel, lavender, marjoram, mint, rosemary, savory, sage and thyme. The caramelized onion gravy is special because it has intense flavor which goes well with bakes, pies and/or nut roast.
Steve Lancaster, Australia/Britain

Heat oven to 400°F/200°C/Gas 6

1 To make the roast, fry the onions in oil and then add the garlic. The onions should brown and there should be some caramelized liquid in the pan.

2 While the onion is cooking, put the peanuts, oats and half of the seeds in a blender and grind them. Mash the beans.

3 Now place all the ingredients in a large bowl and mix thoroughly – it should bind into a thick paste. If

the paste is too dry, add more grated onions and/or carrots.

4 Sprinkle the remaining seeds over the base of an oiled loaf tin. Then transfer the mixture into the tin and press it down with a fork.

5 Bake the roast in the oven for around 30 minutes, until a crust has formed and it is browning.

6 For the sauce, heat the oil and gently cook the onions, followed by the garlic; cover the pan.

7 Once the onions become moist and begin to brown, add the sugar and mushrooms. Continue to cook with the lid on.

8 When the mushrooms have given off their liquid, stir in the sundried tomatoes, tomato paste/purée, stock powder or cube/yeast extract, soy, vinegar and water. Bring to the boil and then simmer until the sauce becomes thick and rich. Add more liquid if/as desired.

Vegeburgers

Macrobiotist Gregory Sams, an American living in Britain, invented the vegeburger in the early 1980s. These are a good standby for barbecues as well as for general munching. They are fairly plain, as people often like to eat them with spicy sauces. This mix has just a little ground coriander which can be omitted, or you can add other herbs and flavorings.

MAKES 12-15

Preparation: 20 minutes
Cooking: 10-15 minutes

1 cup / 200 g green lentils

3 carrots, chopped

1 onion, chopped

2 cloves garlic, chopped

3 slices bread, crumbled

½ tsp ground coriander

2 tbsp parsley

1 tbsp cilantro/coriander

1 egg, beaten

a little flour

salt and pepper

1 Boil the lentils for 15-20 minutes or until just soft. Drain well.

2 Put the carrots, onion, garlic, bread, ground coriander, parsley and cilantro/coriander into a blender and whiz.

3 Now put in the lentils and beaten egg; season and stir well.

4 Form the mix into burgers and lay them on a floured plate to coat each side.

5 Cook on the barbecue, or under a hot broiler/grill, for about 5-7 minutes on each side. Pop the burgers into bread rolls and serve with tomato sauce or other condiments, plus salad.

Vegetable curry

This is a basic vegetable curry, good for a midweek lift. You can pretty much use whatever vegetables you have to hand – the ones below are a guide. For a quicker meal, you can partially cook the potato, carrot and cauliflower first.
Chris Brazier and Pat Tope, Oxford, England

SERVES 4

Preparation: 10 minutes
Cooking: 40 minutes

1 onion, chopped

3 cloves garlic, chopped

1 carrot, sliced finely

1 potato, diced

1 apple, sliced

2 tsp curry powder

1 tsp ground ginger

2 tsp paprika

1 can tomatoes

1-2 tbsp tomato paste/purée

water or bouillon/stock

1 cup / 325 g cauliflower florets, chopped finely

1 can garbanzos/chickpeas, drained

1 tbsp sultanas or raisins

4 hard-boiled eggs, quartered +

oil

salt and pepper

+ optional

1 Heat the oil and sauté the onion for 5 minutes or until it is soft. Then add the garlic, carrot, potato and apple and fry gently for 10 minutes or until beginning to soften.

2 Next, put in the curry powder, ginger and paprika and stir to cook for 1 minute. Add the tomatoes and tomato paste/purée and mix well.

3 Add water or bouillon/stock as required, and season. Stir, and then put in the cauliflower, garbanzos/chickpeas and sultanas or raisins. Bring to the boil, stirring, and then reduce the heat. Cover, and simmer for about 25 minutes or until the vegetables are cooked. Top with quartered eggs, if using.

4 Serve with rice or breads and chutney or cucumber *raita* – thinly sliced cucumber mixed with plain yogurt and a few chopped mint leaves.

Vegetable stir-fry

This has its origins in Chinese cooking. There are many different versions, so feel free to experiment. The point is to have a good mix, and to cook quickly. Best to use groundnut/peanut oil which can take high heat without burning.

<u>S E R V E S   4</u>

Preparation: 20 minutes
Cooking: 20 minutes

1-inch / 2.5-cm piece fresh ginger, chopped

1 cup / 200 g sweetcorn

2 cups / 200 g green beans, chopped into small pieces, or snowpeas/mangetout

1 cup / 100 g sliced mushrooms

½ red bell pepper, diced

1 cup / 250 g cooked rice

4 scallions/spring onions, chopped

2 cups / 200 g bean sprouts

2 tbsp cashew nuts

2 tbsp soy sauce

oil

1 Heat some oil in a wok. Over a high heat, stir-fry the ginger with the sweetcorn, beans, mushrooms and bell pepper for a couple of minutes until they begin to soften.

2 Now put in the cooked rice and scallions/spring onions and stir round to integrate with the other ingredients. Add the bean sprouts, cashews and soy sauce.

3 Stir-fry briskly for a few minutes, adding more soy sauce to taste and serve piping hot.

Dan Zen under a CC License

Veggie fulani pie

My husband and I live in a very remote area of Kwara State, Nigeria. We are two Canadians from Vancouver living and teaching in Oko, both vegetarians. When we first arrived here, we realized that our diet was going to be made up of beans, beans and more beans. So I had to get a bit creative with legumes. This is my recipe for veggie shepherd's pie. The shepherds or herdspeople in Nigeria are Fulani so we have renamed this old classic as veggie fulani pie. You can serve it with the gravy, see below. It's a nice warm dish on those cold Nigerian nights!

Jocelyn and Ryan Sullivan, Nigeria

SERVES 4

Preparation: 15 minutes
Cooking: 45 minutes

1 cup / 200 g lentils (brown or green)

2 cups / 490 ml bouillon/ stock

1 bay leaf

2 carrots, diced

1 pound / 450 g potatoes, chopped and boiled

1 onion, sliced finely

1-2 bell peppers, diced

3 cloves garlic, minced

1 can tomatoes

2-3 tsp oregano

1-2 tsp cumin

1 tsp soy sauce

margarine or butter

oil

salt and pepper

For the gravy:

1 onion or leek, sliced

¼ cup / 25 g flour

2 cups / 490 ml stock

1 tbsp miso or soy sauce

1 tsp maple syrup [+]

butter or margarine

[+] optional

1 Bring the dry lentils, veggie stock and bay leaf to a boil. Simmer until tender, about 20 minutes, adding the carrots about 10 minutes before the end. Add more water if necessary.

2 Sauté the onion and bell peppers; when they are soft, add the garlic and stir to cook for a few more minutes.

3 Add the tomatoes, oregano, cumin, lentils and soy sauce. Stir, and simmer with the lid on for 5 minutes. Add salt and pepper to taste.

5 Mash the potatoes with margarine or butter, salt and pepper.

6 In a baking dish, spoon the lentil mixture onto the bottom. Cover it with the mashed potatoes.

7 Bake for 20 to 30 minutes until the lentils are bubbling and the potatoes are a golden brown.

8 For the gravy, sauté the onion or leek in butter or margarine until translucent. Stir in the flour and cook for 2 minutes, stirring.

9 Now pour in the stock, and stir continuously. Bring to a boil. Reduce heat and simmer for 5 minutes, stirring to remove any lumps.

10 If using miso, mix it with a tablespoon of hot water and then pour it in. If using soy, just add it now, along with the maple syrup if using.

Zucchini/courgettes with herbs and cheese

Everyone who grows zucchini/courgettes probably ends up with a few extra large ones, like marrows. They can be processed into chutneys and pickles, of course, but this simple dish offers a good way to cook them; it's good for a snack lunch.

SERVES 4

Preparation: 10 minutes
Cooking: 25 minutes

2 pounds / 1 kg zucchini/ courgettes, peeled and sliced finely

2 cloves garlic, chopped

1 tsp fennel seeds

2 bay leaves

2 tbsp parsley, chopped

1-2 cups / 100-200 g grated cheddar-type cheese

oil

salt and pepper

1 Place the zucchini/courgette slices in a frying pan and add a very little boiling water. Cover the pan, and parboil the vegetables for a couple of minutes. Drain.

2 Heat the oil in the pan and add the slices, stirring round. Then put in the garlic, fennel seeds and bay leaves. Continue to cook for 10 minutes or until the vegetables are soft and slightly browned. Add the parsley and seasoning, and stir gently to mix.

3 Heat the broiler/grill and transfer the zucchini/courgettes to a heat-proof dish. Scatter the cheese on top and brown under the grill. Serve with crusty bread, potatoes or rice, and salad.

SALADS, SIDE DISHES AND SAUCES

Baked fennel

Fennel looks beautiful – those delicate fronds like tiny palms, and the white/green bulb with its aniseed flavor. This is nice on its own as a light meal, or can be served alongside other dishes. And of course fennel is very tasty, raw, in salads.

SERVES 4

Preparation: 10 minutes
Cooking: 45 minutes

2 bulbs of fennel, trimmed and quartered

1 onion, sliced

1 clove garlic, crushed

1 tbsp tomato paste/purée

1 tsp flour

½ cup / 120 ml bouillon/stock

a few fennel seeds

oil

salt and pepper

Heat oven to 350°F/180°C/Gas 4

1 Blanch the fennel quarters in boiling salted water for 10 minutes; drain and set aside.

2 Sauté the onion in a flameproof pan and then add the garlic, tomato paste/purée and flour. Stir and cook for 1 minute.

3 Next, pour in the bouillon/stock and bring to the boil; season. Put the fennel in now and turn it around to coat with the sauce. Cover with a lid and cook for 30-40 minutes. Check, and baste, from time to time. Sprinkle on fennel seeds before serving.

Beetroot, potato and shallot salad

This has wondrous color, the potatoes turning deep pink as they become infused with beetroot juice. Even people who do not normally like beetroot will enjoy this, I'm sure. The caramelized beet juice gives a sweetness to the salad.

SERVES 4

Preparation: 15 minutes
Cooking: 40 minutes

4 beetroot

4 potatoes, cut into chunks

2 shallots or 1 small red onion, sliced finely

1 tbsp parsley, chopped

olive oil

balsamic vinegar

salt and pepper

Heat oven to 300°F/150°C/Gas 2

1 Boil the beetroot for 30 minutes or until becoming soft. Drain, retaining the liquid. Then remove the peel and cut the beetroot into small chunks.

2 Add the beetroot chunks, potatoes and shallots or onions to the beetroot cooking liquid, and boil for 5-10 minutes. Remove from the heat and leave to stand for some minutes; then drain, again keeping the liquid.

3 Place the vegetables in a bowl, pour some olive oil and balsamic vinegar over the mixture, and add seasoning. Mix well and place in a low oven to keep warm.

4 Now boil the beetroot juice so that it thickens and caramelizes a bit, stirring frequently. Pour this over the vegetables, and sprinkle with parsley before serving warm.

Bread and tomato salad

This Greek, vegan recipe is good for using up old bread
– and it is more delicious than that makes it sound!
Michael York and Denise Salambasis, Oxford, England

SERVES 4-6

Preparation: 5 minutes

6 cups / 300 g old brown bread, broken into chunks and soaked in water (just for a minute or two) then drained

¾ cup / 280 ml olive oil

1 tbsp wine vinegar

1 tbsp fresh or ½ tbsp dried oregano

3-4 tomatoes, chopped finely

3 cloves garlic, crushed

2 tbsp parsley, chopped

10 black olives

salt

1 Mix the bread and half the oregano, vinegar and salt in a bowl.

2 Then add all the other ingredients and mix. Taste and adjust flavorings before serving. Alternatively, you can use a blender but in that case, do not put in the olives until you serve, and do not over-blend; this is best a bit chunky.

visualthinker under a CC License

Buttered zucchini/ courgettes with garlic and lime

When I first encountered zucchini/courgettes I didn't know what to do with them – I loved their rich green color but found their flavor disappointingly bland. Attempts to jazz them up with spices from my Indian repertoire backfired. (Now I find they make lovely fried dumplings mixed with *besan* [chickpea] flour and masala, but that's another story.) Here's a simple dish taught me by a British friend that works a treat.

Dinyar Godrej, Rotterdam, The Netherlands

SERVES 4

Preparation: 2-3 minutes
Cooking: 10 minutes

1 pound / 450 g zucchini/courgettes,
   halved lengthwise and sliced thinly

2 cloves garlic, crushed

1 tbsp chives, chopped

1 tbsp lime juice

butter

salt and pepper

1 Melt a small knob of butter in a pan with a lid and gently soften the garlic in it for a minute or two (take care that it doesn't start to brown). Add the zucchini/ courgettes and season with salt and pepper.

2 Stir well and cook, partially covered, for a further 5-10 minutes or until just done.

3 Add the chives, and lime juice to taste, and leave on the heat for a further minute before serving. Eat with crusty bread or potatoes, or as a side dish.

Chutney

There's something very satisfying about making chutney from abundant garden produce that, one fears, may not be appreciated as a cooked dish. Zucchini/courgettes, apples, carrots, beans, tomatoes – these are some of the items that make a good brew.

MAKES 8-12 JARS

Preparation: 30-60 minutes
Cooking: 90 minutes

6 cups / 2 kg zucchini/courgettes, chopped

4 onions, chopped

4 cups / 600 g beans, chopped – use any green beans

3 cups / 450 g carrots, chopped finely

4½ cups / 450 g apples, chopped

2 cups / 300 g raisins/sultanas

2½ cups / 600 ml malt vinegar

1 tsp fresh ginger, grated

½ tsp cinnamon

6 allspice, ground

5 cups / 500 g brown sugar

salt

1 Put the vegetables in a large pan with the vinegar and spices, put the lid on and bring to a boil.

2 Simmer the contents, stirring from time to time, until they have mulched down and are becoming integrated.

3 Now add the sugar, plus salt if/ as required, and stir well to dissolve. Adjust the flavorings and continue to cook for about an hour until everything is soft.

4 Once you have the consistency and flavor you want, turn off the heat and leave the chutney to cool a little before bottling in clean, warmed jam jars.

Coconut rice

The coconut milk and cinnamon give a rich, delicate flavor to the rice and as such it becomes a delicious, fragrant accompaniment to other dishes.

<u>SERVES 4</u>

Preparation: 5 minutes

Cooking: 20 minutes

1½ cups / 300 g basmati rice

3 cloves

4 tbsp raisins or sultanas

1 can coconut milk

1 stick cinnamon

3 cardamom pods, left whole

½ cup / 60 g cashew nuts

salt

1 Cook the rice with the cloves, cardamom pods and raisins or sultanas in boiling water for 10 minutes or until the rice is just becoming soft and the raisins or sultanas are swollen.

2 Transfer the rice mix to a sieve and drain; then rinse with cold water.

3 Now put the rice mix back into the pan and add the coconut milk, cinnamon stick and cashew nuts plus a little salt.

4 Cook very gently for a further 10-15 minutes, to incorporate all the flavors, before serving.

Copper Penny carrots

A good friend of mine gave me this recipe a long time ago. It makes a large salad and is good to have on hand for those warm barbecue days and extra company.

Henriette Faber, Kelowna, British Columbia, Canada

SERVES 4 - 6

Preparation: 10 minutes
Cooking: 15 minutes

8 carrots, sliced finely

1 green pepper, chopped finely

1 onion, sliced finely

¾ cup / 175 g sugar

1 tsp Worcestershire sauce

1 can condensed tomato soup *

½ cup / 120 ml olive oil

½ cup / 120 ml vinegar

¼ cup / 60 ml cider vinegar

1 tsp dry mustard

salt and pepper

* If you cannot find this, use ordinary canned tomato soup or 6 tbsp tomato ketchup.

1 Cook carrots in boiling water for about 8 minutes. They should still be crunchy. Arrange layers of carrots, pepper and onion in a container with a tight-fitting lid.

2 Combine all the other ingredients and boil, stirring, until thoroughly blended. Pour the marinade over the carrots.

3 Cover, and chill overnight. This will keep in the refrigerator for a week. Leftover marinade can be used as a dressing over tossed salad.

Corn fritters

Some version of these turns up wherever there is sweetcorn/*mielies*
– US, Mexico, South Africa. But it's not surprising as they are
delicious and go well with lots of dishes.

1 cup / 225 g maize/sweetcorn

½ cup / 50 g self-rising flour

2 eggs, beaten

¼ tsp chili powder

2 tbsp grated cheese ⁺

oil

salt

⁺ optional

1 Mix all the ingredients together in
a bowl.

2 Heat some oil in a non-stick
pan and when it is very hot, put
in spoonfuls of the mixture. Turn
down the heat a little and then cook
to brown on both sides and serve
immediately with salsa or sweet chili
sauce (see p 200).

Broad bean salad

The broad bean season is fairly short, but can be memorable. Here's a tasty
way to serve them – either as a starter or a side dish.

1 pound / 490 g broad beans

4-6 cloves garlic

1 tbsp fennel, chopped

2 tsp lemon juice

oil

salt and pepper

1 Cook the beans together with the
garlic cloves in a little water until soft.

2 Drain and transfer to a serving dish.
Add the fennel and squeeze on some
lemon juice.

3 Pour a little olive oil over, and
season. Mix and then serve hot.

Crunchy garlicky potatoes

This way of cooking potatoes is inspired by south Indian flavors and is an unusual and surprising dish – well worth springing on your guests. People with peanut allergies can leave the nuts out and if you can't find the gorgeously aromatic curry leaves at your local Asian grocer, you can also omit these. Use the white *urid dal* for this recipe, not the black one which still has its husk. The potatoes stay soft in this dish – it's the lentils and peanuts that add the crunch. If you can only find dried curry leaves, then soak them in a little water beforehand.

Dinyar Godrej, Rotterdam, The Netherlands

SERVES 3-4

Preparation: 10 minutes
Cooking: 20 minutes

3 cups / 500 g waxy potatoes, cut into thin chips

1 tbsp urid dal (white lentils), soaked in a little water for 15 minutes or so, then drained

1 tsp mustard seeds

3-4 cloves of garlic, sliced

1 dried red chili, broken in two

pinch of asafetida *

10-15 fresh curry leaves

1 tbsp raw peanuts

oil

salt

* Asafetida is a highly aromatic resin, available from specialty or Asian shops.

1 Boil some water and blanch the potatoes for a couple of minutes. Drain.

2 Coat the bottom of a (non-stick) frying pan with a thin layer of oil and heat up. Throw in the urid dal, mustard seeds, garlic, chili and asafetida and stir rapidly for a minute until fragrant.

3 Add the curry leaves, stir for a few seconds, and then tip in the potatoes and peanuts. Stir for a further minute or two and add salt to taste. Now turn down the heat to medium low and cook for a further 10 minutes or so, stirring regularly, until the potatoes are done.

Dobi – spinach and tomato

I was born in Zimbabwe so this spinach and tomato dish reminds me of my childhood there. *Dobi* is traditionally served with *sadza*, the maize meal staple eaten in Zimbabwe, also known as *pap* or *ugali* in various parts of Africa. *Sadza* is similar to Italian polenta. However, as it is not so easy to make and the maize meal is not always available [especially in today's Zimbabwe], I have also served the peanut butter spinach on crackers as a starter. I recently took it to an international party where everyone was asked to bring a dish from their country, and the plate was polished off in no time.
Laura Brown

SERVES 2

Preparation: 10 minutes
Cooking: 10 minutes

1 onion, chopped

1 can tomatoes, or 4-6 fresh, chopped

1-2 cloves garlic, chopped

1-2 tsp mixed herbs, such as parsley and thyme *

¼-½ fresh green chili, de-seeded and chopped ⁺

2 cups / 250 g spinach/ spinach beet/chard, chopped

1 tbsp peanut butter

oil

salt and pepper

* Fresh herbs are best if you have them.
⁺ optional

1 Fry the chopped onion on medium heat until brown.

2 Add the tomatoes, garlic, herbs; season to taste. Spice it up with chili if you dare! Simmer for about 5 minutes.

3 Now put in the spinach and simmer until it is tender. Finally add peanut butter – you can add more or less according to your preference. Stir round to mix the ingredients and then serve.

CPWF Basin Focal Project under a CC License

Early zucchini/ courgette salad

Early zucchini have great flavor; you can cook them with sprouting broccoli or young carrots. The seeds taste better if you toast them first. Heat a heavy pan with no oil and put them in when the pan is hot. Stir and shake as they toast, for 2-3 minutes. Remove them from the pan straight away when ready. You could also try this with *Lee's salad dressing* (see p 182).

SERVES 4

Preparation: 10 minutes
Cooking: 10 minutes

4 small zucchini/courgettes, sliced lengthwise very finely

1 cup / 175 g sprouting broccoli

4 tbsp cream or yogurt

2 tsp balsamic vinegar

1 tbsp sesame oil

2 tbsp pumpkin seeds, toasted

2 tbsp sunflower seeds, toasted

a few lettuce or salad leaves, torn

salt and pepper

1 Boil the broccoli for a few minutes and then drain and leave to cool.

2 Mix together the balsamic vinegar with the sesame oil. Then add the cream or yogurt, plus salt and pepper to taste.

3 In a serving bowl, mix the lettuce with the zucchini/courgettes and broccoli. Pour the dressing over, mix with the salad, and then sprinkle the seeds on top.

Eggplant/aubergine with spicy potatoes

A tasty dish from the Moluccas, in Indonesia. These were formerly known as the Spice Islands, and were the source of many spices, such as cloves and nutmeg, that were highly prized in Europe. Some of the earliest big companies, such as the Dutch East India Company, set up in the early 17th century, were involved in trading such commodities.

SERVES 2-4

Preparation: 10 minutes
Cooking: 20 minutes

1 eggplant/aubergine, diced

2 potatoes, diced and parboiled

1 onion, sliced

½ tsp chili powder

½ tsp mustard seeds

½ tsp turmeric

**½-inch / 1-cm piece fresh
ginger root, chopped**

lemon/lime juice

oil

salt

Rosino under a CC License

1 Heat the oil in a pan and cook the onion until it is clear and soft.

2 After that put in the chili, mustard seeds, turmeric, ginger and salt. Cook on a gentle heat, stirring to mix well. Then turn up the heat, add the eggplant/aubergine and parboiled potatoes and brown them, turning to prevent them catching.

3 Add a little water to cover the base of the pan, put the lid on and cook gently for 10 minutes or so until the vegetables are tender and the liquid is absorbed.

SALADS, SIDE DISHES & SAUCES 177

Fiery spinach with chilies

Here's a sparky spinach recipe, from Penang. I often make this and it's good!
Mahmuda Fazal, Penang, Malaysia

Preparation: 10 minutes
Cooking: 15 minutes

2 pounds / 1 kg spinach, finely sliced

1 onion, chopped

3-4 cloves garlic, chopped

1-inch / 2.5-cm piece of fresh ginger, chopped

½ tsp turmeric

1-2 green chilies

juice of 1 lemon

oil

1 Heat the oil and then add the onion, garlic and ginger.

2 When the onion becomes transparent, add the stems of spinach and the turmeric; stir well to combine the ingredients.

3 When nearly cooked put in the spinach leaves and whole chilies. As the leaves wilt, sprinkle in a little salt to taste. Add a little bit of water just to keep it moist but the aim is for the spinach to cook in its own juice.

4 Squeeze on some lemon juice before serving, with hot chapatis.

Jeera aloo – potatoes with cumin

Potatoes are cooked in a variety of ways in India and are tremendously popular. This simple dish is easy to make while cooking something else as it needs very little attention. You can cook it quicker over a higher heat, but then you have to watch over it more. *Asafetida* is a completely unique and highly aromatic resin. A little goes a long way, so don't be tempted to be generous with it. It is best to buy the lumpy form as that is the purest version, but you can also get it ready powdered. *Dhansak masala* is a wonderfully aromatic composite spice mixture – but if you don't feel like buying a pack just to try out this dish use another Indian curry powder or masala mix, preferably a hot blend, or just add a little extra red powder if using a milder masala.

Dinyar Godrej, Rotterdam, The Netherlands

SERVES 2-3

Preparation: 2 minutes
Cooking: 30 minutes

1 pound / 450 g waxy potatoes, diced

1 tsp cumin seeds

asafetida *

½ tsp turmeric

1 tsp dhansak masala **

oil

salt

* A piece the size of a grain of rice, powdered, or a pinch of the ready powdered version. See introduction above for more about asafetida.
** See introduction, above.

1 Boil some water and parboil the potatoes for 2-3 minutes. Drain thoroughly.

2 Coat the bottom of a (non-stick) frying pan with a thin layer of oil and heat. (Choose a size of pan in which the potatoes will fit snugly.) Add the cumin and asafetida and after a few seconds, add the potatoes and stir. Sprinkle with turmeric and salt and stir to coat the potatoes. Cook until they have dried out and then lower the heat.

3 Let the potatoes cook on a low heat stirring every 5 minutes or so, until they start to get crispy. Now add the dhansak masala, stir, let it cook gently for a further 2 minutes and then serve.

Lee's salad dressing

This is a salad dressing I've been making for at least 20 years, and it's always a hit. It's great as a dressing, but can go onto steamed vegetables and rice, or many other dishes. For the oil, use olive, canola or whatever you use, and add as much or as little as you want.

Lee Bartell, Provincetown, Massachusetts, US

MAKES 6 SERVINGS

Preparation: 5 minutes

3 cloves garlic

1-inch/2.5-cm piece of ginger

2 tbsp lemon juice

2 tbsp tamari/soy sauce

2 tbsp tahini

oil

Put the ingredients into a blender or food processor – something that will chop it all up and blend it well.

Lentil salad with feta cheese and vegetables

There are many lentil salads, but I like this one based on a *Good Housekeeping* recipe. It uses *Puy* (also called green or blue) lentils. These have a good flavor and plenty of 'mouth feel' to make a substantial dish. This salad is best served at room temperature, so if you make it the day before and keep it in the fridge, remember to take it out at least a couple of hours before you are serving it.

Andrew Hine, London, England

1 cup / 225 g Puy lentils

1 carrot, sliced finely

1 leek, sliced finely

1 stick celery, sliced finely

1 onion, sliced finely

1 cup / 200 g snowpeas/ mangetout

1 cup / 200 g French beans

1 cup / 125 g asparagus tips

1 cup /125 g feta cheese

1 quart / 1 liter bouillon/ vegetable stock

2-3 bay leaves

1-2 cloves garlic, crushed

¼ tsp paprika

pinch of cayenne

oil

juice of 1 lemon

salt and pepper *

* Feta cheese is quite salty so you may not need additional salt.

1 First, heat some oil in a pan and then sauté the onion, followed by the carrot, leek and celery. Then add the lentils and bay leaves and stir round before pouring in the stock. Bring to the boil, cover the pan and simmer for about 30 minutes, until tender.

2 Stir from time to time and add more liquid if necessary to complete cooking, so that the lentils are soft and have absorbed the liquid.

3 While that is happening, boil some water and cook the snowpeas/mangetout for 3 minutes or so. Remove, and then cook the French beans and later the asparagus in the same way. Remove and drain well, or pat dry with kitchen towel.

4 Make a dressing by mixing together some oil, the lemon juice, garlic, paprika, cayenne and seasoning.

5 When the lentil mix is ready, drain and place in a large bowl. Leave to cool for 5 minutes or so before pouring on the dressing; stir lightly to distribute. Set aside to cool.

6 When ready, stir in the green vegetables and crumble the feta cheese on top before serving.

Mediterranean salad

The kind of ingredients found in North Africa – in fact, virtually anywhere around the Mediterranean.

SERVES 4

Preparation: 10 minutes

2 red peppers, de-seeded, diced finely

4-6 tomatoes, chopped finely

5-inch/12-cm cucumber, diced finely

1 onion or 2 scallions/spring onions, sliced finely

12 green olives, pitted and chopped

2 hard-boiled eggs, quartered

2 tbsp basil, chopped

2 tbsp cilantro/coriander, chopped

¼ tsp ground cumin

vinegar

oil

salt and pepper

Put everything into a salad bowl and toss; serve with pita bread or rice.

Nettle tagliatelle verde

My friend's horse Harley and mine, Copper, have to be shod every six weeks or so. Their farrier or blacksmith, Roger, visits with his mobile forge to do the work. He's a great outdoors person, loves survival kayaking and living off the land in extreme conditions. This is based on a recipe he makes with the kids he takes on outdoor trips.

SERVES 4

*Preparation: 30 minutes +
30 minutes
Cooking: 10 minutes*

1 cup / 100 g young
    nettle tops, chopped *

3 cups / 300 g strong
    bread flour

3 eggs

3 tsp olive oil

salt

* You can use spinach instead
if you prefer.

1 Boil the nettle tops till soft in a little water, and then squeeze to drain well.

2 On the worktop, pile the flour in a dome shape, and then form a well in the center. Put in the eggs and a little salt.

3 Mix together with a fork, and then knead with your hands. When the mixture is smooth, add the well-drained nettle tops and knead them in gently. Set the dough aside to rest for 30 minutes.

4 Now divide the dough into 3 or 4 pieces. Flatten each piece and then, on a floured surface, roll it out very thinly. When ready, slice the pasta with a knife or pizza wheel into long strips to form tagliatelle, about ¼ inch/½ cm wide. Allow the strips to dry slowly before use.

Rosemary pesto

A variation on the basil-and-pine nuts classic, and very good. Use the young tips of the rosemary if you can, as these are more tender.

Preparation: 10 minutes

1 cup / 150 g cashews

1 tbsp fresh rosemary (leaves only)

2 cloves garlic

2 tbsp olive oil

1 cup / 50 g cheddar cheese, grated

1 cup / 50 g yogurt

lemon juice to taste

salt and pepper to taste

Put all the ingredients into a blender to make a smooth paste. Store in a screw-top jar in the fridge.

Papas a la Huancaína – Peruvian potatoes

When I used to leave Peru, at the airport I would have my favorite Peruvian foods that I would have to go without when I got back home: *Lucama** ice cream, and *Papas a la Huancaína*. Since my meal basically was an appetizer and a dessert, the waitstaff gave me deservedly strange looks. *Papas a la Huancaína* is a key dish of Criollan food (the food from Lima) and one of the most beloved. It is a good side dish or starter – basically cooked potatoes served with a cream made with cheese and *aji* (chili).

Abby Shuler

* A South American fruit often used to flavor ice cream.

SERVES 4

Preparation: 10 minutes
Cooking: 10 minutes

6 potatoes, chopped into slices, boiled

2-4 green chilies, de-seeded

1 tbsp sugar

2 egg yolks

2 cups / 500 g fresh cheese, such as ricotta

½-1 cup / 120-240 ml milk

juice of 2-3 lemons

1 tbsp oil

lettuce leaves

3 hard-boiled eggs, cut in half

10 olives

1 tbsp parsley, chopped

salt and pepper

1 Boil the chilies with the sugar in a little water for a minute or so. Then remove the chilies (discard the water) and blend them with the egg-yolks and cheese. Add some milk, lemon juice and oil to make a thick coating sauce. Season.

2 Arrange the lettuce leaves on a plate and place the cooked potatoes on them. Spoon the sauce over, and decorate with the hard-boiled eggs, olives and parsley.

lanz under a CC License

Potato, bean and olive salad

The sweet sauce is made from boiled sweet pumpkin in grape must (the pulpy juice of grapes destined for wine) producing small firm chunks in a dark sweet winey-tasting caramel-like sauce. You can obtain it at www.tienda.com/food/products/ – or use honey instead. This recipe was given to me by my daughter after her travels in Spain. It is absolutely delicious and very simple and fast to make.

Margaret Matthews, Perth, Australia

SERVES 4

Preparation: 10 minutes
Cooking: 10 minutes

4-6 potatoes, diced

20 green beans, chopped

2 cups kalamata olives, pitted and chopped

3 tbsp olive oil

3 tbsp lemon juice

3 tbsp sweet sauce (see above), or use honey

extra oil for cooking

1 Boil the potatoes; drain well.

2 Heat some oil in a pan and lightly fry the potatoes until golden.

3 While the potatoes are cooking, boil the beans and drain when ready.

4 Mix the beans and potatoes in a bowl with the olives.

5 Stir the lemon juice, olive oil and sweet sauce or honey together and pour over the salad; mix well and serve hot.

Potato, lemon and parsley mix

Another tasty Greek recipe, one that we often have when we visit relatives near Salonika.

Michael York and Denise Salambasis, Oxford, England

1 pound / 450 g potatoes, chopped
2-3 cloves garlic, crushed
juice of 1-2 lemons
¼ cup / 60 ml olive oil
2-4 tbsp parsley, very finely chopped
salt

1 Boil the potatoes and when soft, drain, and then mix with the garlic while still hot. Make into a smooth paste (using a processor is best).

2 Then gradually add all the other ingredients and mix well.

3 This side dish can be served straight away hot or can be cooled and kept in the fridge to serve cold. It's nice decorated with a twisted lemon slice or some olives.

Shadowgate under a CC License

Red bell pepper bake

Red vegetables look great on the table with salads and other dishes, and the flavor of baked red peppers and tomatoes is hard to beat.

2 red bell peppers or
    pimientos

2-4 tomatoes, quartered

2 cloves garlic, crushed

2 tsp dried oregano

1-2 tbsp parsley, chopped

oil

salt and pepper

Heat oven to 400°F/200°C/Gas 6

1 Grill the peppers or pimientos, left whole, turning frequently so they do not burn.

2 When they are ready, let them cool and then remove the stalk and seeds. Slice the peppers lengthwise.

3 Arrange the peppers and tomatoes in a baking dish. Add the garlic, herbs and seasoning.

4 Bake for 15-20 minutes and either serve warm or cold.

Roast *kumara*/sweet potato and garbanzo/chickpea salad

This recipe reminds me of relaxed summers in New Zealand, as it is a perfect salad accompaniment for a barbecue. It is a variation of a recipe my sister used to make before I moved over to the UK for a few years, so it reminds me of family and friends and good times back in New Zealand.

This is a fantastic, filling, summer salad – it could be a good snack meal for two people – which can be served hot or cold depending on preference. It's also great for lunch the next day. In New Zealand we call sweet potato 'kumara' and there are several different varieties; my preference for the recipe is the gold variety, also available in the UK but called sweet potato. The salad is also dairy-, gluten-, egg-, and soy-free so is perfect for people with allergies or food intolerances.

Rebecca Sinclair, New Zealand

SERVES 2-4

Preparation: 5 minutes
Cooking: 25 minutes

2 sweet potatoes, chopped

1 tsp cumin seeds

1 tbsp honey

2 cloves garlic, chopped

½ tsp cumin powder

½ tsp cinnamon

1 bell pepper

2-3 tbsp sundried tomatoes, roughly chopped

1 can garbanzos/ chickpeas, drained

1 tbsp pine nuts

2 tbsp cilantro/ coriander, chopped

oil

Heat oven to 350°F/180°C/Gas 4

1 Put the chopped sweet potatoes into a bowl and coat with 1 tablespoon of oil, the cumin seeds and the honey. Mix well.

2 Turn the mixture out onto a baking sheet, and cook for about 20 minutes, until soft. You can put the whole bell pepper alongside at the same time to roast, or else char the skin by holding in the flame of a gas cooker, turning often. Whichever method, when it is ready, leave to cool and then slice.

3 Now put about 2 tablespoons of oil into a pan on a low heat and when hot add the garlic, cumin and cinnamon. Stir briefly.

4 The bell pepper, sundried tomatoes, and garbanzos/chickpeas go in now. Stir for a few minutes to coat with the spice mixture.

5 When ready, turn into a bowl and mix in the sweet potatoes. Sprinkle the pine nuts and fresh cilantro/coriander on top.

Salsa

The Spanish word 'salsa', meaning sauce, is also used for the salsa dance, in the sense of flavor or style. It usually connotes the hot spiciness that is found in Mexican cooking. The sauce usually contains bell peppers, onions, tomatoes, garlic, cilantro/coriander, oil and vinegar. But of course you can experiment.

1 red onion, sliced finely

3 cloves garlic, crushed

1 red chili, de-seeded, chopped finely

1 can tomatoes

1 red bell pepper, chopped finely

2 tbsp cilantro/coriander, chopped

lemon or lime juice

olive oil

salt and pepper

Put everything into a blender and whiz until smooth. Adjust to taste and keep in a bottle in the fridge.

Sweet chili sauce

I started to make this recipe as a skint student. In midsummer, chili, garlic and galangal/ginger are at their cheapest, meaning that a couple of dollars in the local markets and a few hours' work in the kitchen kept me in chili sauce all year long. The added advantage is that a spare bottle with a home-made label works well as an emergency gift when required. Recycled flip-top bottles such as Grolsch beer are ideal.

Adam Henderson, Sydney, Australia

SERVES 4

Preparation: 10 minutes
Cooking: 15 minutes

¾ cup / 100 g bird's eye or long red chilies*, de-seeded

1¼ cups / 200 g sultanas

2 tbsp fresh galangal or ginger, chopped

8 cloves garlic

3 tbsp soy sauce

1¼ cups / 300 ml water

1¼ cups / 300 ml white cider vinegar

1 cup / 250 g brown sugar

* Note that bird's eye chilies are hot; you could use long red chilies which are less fiery.

1 Put the chilies, sultanas, garlic, galangal/ginger and soy sauce into a blender and purée them, adding water as required to develop an even blend/mix.

2 Spoon the purée into a saucepan, add the vinegar and sugar, and bring to a simmer.

3 Cover, and continue to simmer until the mixture has reduced, stirring from time to time to prevent sticking.

4 Leave to cool, and then bottle in sterilized and re-sealable jars or bottles. The sauce will keep for six months and the flavor develops with age.

Soaked cucumber salad

Versions of this salad are found in Southeast Asia. Toasting the sesame seeds first for this recipe gives them a nuttier flavor.

<u>S E R V E S   4 - 6</u>

Preparation: 10 minutes

1-2 cucumbers*, peeled

½ cup / 120 ml white wine or cider vinegar

1 tbsp sesame seeds

1 tbsp sesame oil

1 onion, sliced very finely

2 cloves garlic, sliced very finely

1 tsp turmeric

1-2 tsp sugar

salt

* Use one long or two short cucumbers.

Rosino under a CC License

1 Cut the cucumber/s into 2-inch/5-cm pieces, and then cut the pieces again into very thin lengthwise sticks.

2 Now put the sticks into a pan with the vinegar and salt. Add a little water to cover, heat and simmer for a few minutes until the cucumber is slightly tender and transparent. Drain, keeping the liquid, and let the cucumber cool. Set aside.

3 Next, heat a pan with no oil and toast the sesame seeds until they begin to jump and turn golden. Then turn off the heat and let them cool.

4 In the same pan, heat a little sesame oil and sauté the onion until golden; then put in the garlic. When ready, remove from the pan and set aside.

5 For the dressing, pour in the remaining oil, add the turmeric, sugar and half the drained vinegar liquid. Stir this over a gentle heat until the sugar is dissolved. Add the onion and garlic and heat them through; sprinkle in salt to taste.

6 Arrange cucumber pieces in a salad bowl and pour over the dressing. Mix well and then scatter the sesame seeds on top. Serve warm or cold.

Spinach and ginger

I have fond childhood memories of my mother making this for me and telling me about its beneficial health effects! It is foolproof, with easy-to-buy ingredients and very healthy. Serve with white jasmine/basmati rice.
Jenny Ai-Ling Lo, Penang, Malaysia

SERVES 4

Preparation: 10 minutes
Cooking: 10 minutes

2 pounds / 800 g fresh spinach, chopped

2-3 tbsp peanut/groundnut or olive oil

4 tbsp fresh ginger, finely chopped

splash of soy sauce

pinch chili powder, or ½ tsp chopped fresh chili, de-seeded

pepper

1 Heat the wok over a high heat, add the oil when very hot and slightly smoking, add the ginger and stir-fry for 12-15 seconds or until cooked but still slightly crispy. Now splash in the soy sauce.

2 Next, put in the spinach and stir-fry for 1-2 minutes so that it blends with the ginger, oil and sauce.

3 When the spinach has wilted to a third of its size, add lots of pepper and continue to stir-fry briefly to combine the ingredients well before serving.

Swiss chard with potatoes and tomatoes

This is a good accompaniment to many dishes; chard has a lovely earthy flavor.

SERVES 4

Preparation: 10 minutes
Cooking: 10 minutes

2 pounds / 1 kg chard, chopped, with the stalks removed to use separately

1-2 tomatoes, chopped

2 potatoes, chopped

2 cloves garlic

¼ tsp ground cumin

¼ green chili, de-seeded, chopped finely

oil

salt and pepper

1 Boil the potatoes with the chard stalks until soft, about 5 minutes. Drain.

2 Heat a little oil in a large pan and gently sauté the potatoes and chard stalks. Add the tomatoes and continue to cook before putting in the cumin and seasoning, stir well.

3 After a couple of minutes, turn up the heat and add the chopped chard leaves. Stir and cook until the leaves have wilted; serve at once.

Turnip treat

You can vary the proportions to suit your taste, and according to what you have around. This is a pleasant mix of root vegetables and green herbs. It makes a warm, mild-tasting accompaniment to other dishes, or stands as a dish on its own served with rice or bread and a salad.

SERVES 4

Preparation: 10 minutes
Cooking: 25 minutes

1 turnip, peeled and chopped

2 carrots, peeled and chopped

2 potatoes, diced

1 onion, sliced

¼ tsp turmeric

1 clove garlic, crushed

½ tsp ground coriander

1 tbsp chives, chopped

2 tbsp parsley, chopped

oil

salt and pepper

Heat the oven to 375°F/190°C/Gas 5

1 Boil the turnip and the carrots with the onion in enough liquid to cover, until they are soft. Drain, and keep the liquid. Boil the potatoes in the liquid until soft, and then drain and set aside, keeping a little of the cooking liquid.

2 Place the turnip, carrots and onion in a blender (or mash with a potato masher), adding some of the cooking liquid as required. Flavor with the turmeric, and salt and pepper. Turn out onto a shallow oven-proof dish.

3 Now mash the potatoes with the garlic, coriander, chives and half the parsley, adding a little of the retained cooking water as required.

4 Spoon the potato on top of the turnip mixture, and smooth the top with a fork. Drizzle a little cooking oil on top to help it brown. Bake for 15 minutes or so and scatter on the remaining parsley before serving.

Winter garden salad

This was made from bits and pieces, most of which were still in the ground in December. Fennel is susceptible to frost so may not survive each year this late. The winter radishes are less hot than their summer counterparts, and go well in this dish – but summer radishes are fine also. The dish is best served warm, and if you can leave it to soak for 30 minutes or so before eating, this gives better flavor.

SERVES 4

Preparation: 5 minutes
Cooking: 45 minutes

1 pound / 450 g beetroot

2 radishes, sliced

1 red onion, sliced finely

2 fennel fronds, chopped

1 apple, sliced

1 tbsp honey or sugar

1 tbsp boiling water

oil

1 tbsp vinegar

salt and pepper

1 Start by cooking the beetroot for about 30 minutes until soft. Drain and leave to cool. When ready, remove the peel and cut into slices.

2 In a salad bowl, mix the beetroot with the radishes, onion, fennel and apple.

3 Now dissolve the honey or sugar in the boiling water; then add the oil and vinegar, and seasoning. Mix well before pouring over the salad and then combine all the ingredients.

DESSERTS, DRINKS AND CAKES

Banana cake

Bananas are a main cash crop for many regions, especially Latin America and the Caribbean but also West Africa and the Philippines. The world's biggest banana exporter is Ecuador.

1½ cups / 200 g flour

¾ cup / 175 g brown sugar

1 tsp baking soda

1 tsp baking powder

¼ tsp cinnamon

3 eggs, beaten

3 ripe bananas, mashed

3 tbsp sultanas

2 tbsp chopped walnuts +

2 tbsp margarine

salt

+ optional

Heat oven to 350°F/180°C/Gas 4

1 To start, sift the flour together with baking soda and baking powder and a little salt into a bowl.

2 In a larger bowl, cream the margarine and sugar, then add the beaten eggs a little at a time. Add the flour mix alternately with some of the mashed bananas and then put in the sultanas and walnuts, if using. Stir gently to mix.

3 Put the mixture into a greased and floured loaf pan. Bake for about 40-45 minutes, or until a skewer inserted into the cake comes out clean. Remove from oven and leave in the cake pan for 15 minutes. Turn out onto a wire rack to finish cooling.

robin.elaine under a CC License

Cheesecake with lime and ginger

Lime and ginger – Caribbean tastes. This recipe has become very popular in our household and there are never any left-overs. Traidcraft's version uses fair-trade stem ginger cookies, but ordinary ones work fine. If you want to add a flourish you can decorate with grated dark chocolate.

Sarah Poulter, Brighton, England

SERVES 4 - 6

Preparation: 10 minutes
Cooking: 2 minutes

2 cups / 225 g ginger cookies, crushed *

¼ cup / 60 g butter or margarine

2 tbsp icing sugar or to taste

4 cups / 500 g mascarpone cheese

grated zest and juice of 2 limes

dark chocolate +

* Crush with the end of a rolling pin.
+ optional

1 Begin by melting the butter or margarine in a pan. When ready, add the crunched ginger biscuits and mix well.

2 Spoon this mixture into a flan dish or spring cake tin and smooth the surface. Chill for 30 minutes.

3 Next, mix the icing sugar and mascarpone in a bowl; add the lime zest and juice and adjust to taste.

4 Spread this over the cookie base and chill in the fridge for a further 30 minutes.

5 If desired, grate on some dark chocolate before serving.

Crunchy crumble

Use any mixture of seasonal fruit – my favorite is apple and blackberry or apple and quince. It is a good way of using up windfall apples.

Make a crumble as normal but instead of half the flour use jumbo oats. Also very nice with ground almonds or any chopped nuts. Sprinkle a bit of sugar and cinnamon on top. Bake quite high for about an hour. Use non-dairy fat if you want to serve to vegans.

Helen Beinart, Oxford, England

<u>SERVES 6</u>

Preparation: 15 minutes
Cooking: 45 minutes

Enough apples to produce
  6 cups / 600 g chopped apples

1 cup / 125 g blackberries

1 cup / 100 g plain flour

¾ cup / 100 g jumbo oats

¾ cup / 125 g brown sugar

½ cup / 90 g butter or margarine

cinnamon

Heat the oven to 180°C/350°F/Gas 4

1 Place the flour, oats and sugar in a large bowl and mix well.

2 Cut the butter or margarine into the mix, and then rub it in with your fingertips to make a mixture like rough breadcrumbs.

3 Spoon the fruit mixture into an oven-proof dish (sprinkle on a little sugar if the fruit is very sour) and then spoon over the crumble mixture, with some cinnamon on top.

4 Bake in the oven for 40-45 minutes until the crumble is browned and the fruit mixture bubbling. Serve with cream or yogurt.

Dairy-free tiramisù

This is adapted from the popular dessert served in Italy. It is special because it is simple to make but rich and delicious – and vegan. Instead of making or using sponge fingers, you can substitute chocolate or other cake – it's a great way of using up cake which is beginning to dry out.

Steve Lancaster, England

SERVES 6-8

Preparation: 30 minutes
Cooking: 25 minutes

For the sponge fingers:

5 cups / 500 g plain flour

1⅓ cups / 300 g sugar

1 tbsp egg replacer *

1 tsp salt

2 tsp baking powder

⅓ cup / 80 ml vinegar

1½ cups / 360 ml soy milk

1 cup / 240 ml sunflower oil

2-4 drops vanilla essence

1 cup / 240 ml cold black coffee

* Vegan egg replacement powder, available from health food shops.

For the custard:

1⅔ cups / 400 ml soy milk

2 tbsp sugar

3 tbsp cornstarch

3 tbsp cocoa

2-4 drops vanilla essence

For the cream:

⅔ cup / 150ml soy milk

⅛ cup / 30 ml maple syrup or apple juice

2-4 drops vanilla essence

2 tbsp icing sugar

1¼ cups / 300 ml sunflower oil

Heat oven to 350°F/180°C/Gas 4

1 First make the sponge fingers. To do this, oil a baking tray (approx 6 inch x 12 inch/15 cm x 30 cm) and line with baking paper.

2 In a bowl, mix the flour, sugar, egg replacer, salt and baking powder. Then add in the vinegar, soy milk, oil and vanilla essence. Stir well and then spoon the mixture onto the baking sheet.

3 Cook for about 25 minutes until golden; a skewer should come out cleanly. Leave to cool before cutting into finger shapes. Then arrange some to cover the bottom of an ovenproof dish and pour half of the coffee on top (you will use the rest of the sponge fingers later).

4 To make the custard, heat the soy milk and add the sugar. Mix the

cornstarch with a little cold water to form a smooth paste, and add this to the milk. Pour a bit of the milk on to the cocoa in a cup and stir to make a smooth paste; then transfer this to the pan of milk. Stir.

5 When the custard is almost boiling, remove the pan from the heat. Leave to cool and then spoon the custard over the sponge fingers. Then place another layer of sponge fingers on top. Pour over the remaining coffee.

6 For the cream, use a hand-held stick blender. Whiz the soy milk, maple syrup or apple juice, icing sugar and vanilla, slowly pouring in the sunflower oil, until the mixture becomes thick. Spread this cream over the sponge fingers. If desired, you can add chocolate shavings and/or a few raspberries on top.

Elderflower drink

The flowers taste best picked early on a sunny day, and speed is crucial: they should be used straight after picking. Elder bushes are ubiquitous in Britain, and are also found in other temperate places of the world, including parts of Australia and Canada. Make sure you have plenty of clean, screw-top bottles ready before you begin. It will keep for about a month in the fridge.

SERVES 4

Preparation: 15 minutes
Cooking: 20 minutes + leave to stand for 24 hours

2 gallons / 8 liters boiling water

5 cups / 1.25 kg sugar

12 elderflower heads

4 lemons, 2 for juice, and 2 sliced

4 tbsp mild white wine vinegar

1 Place the sugar in a large mixing bowl and pour on the boiling water; stir well to dissolve.

2 Allow it to cool a little and then add the elderflowers, juice of the two lemons, slices of the other two and the vinegar.

3 Cover with a cloth and leave for a day.

4 When ready, strain with a fine sieve or muslin cloth, squeezing the flowers as you do to release more flavor.

5 Using a funnel, pour into clean screw-top bottles, and store in the fridge or cool place. It will be ready in about 3 days to a week.

Gaajar halwa – carrot fudge

I remember eating this carrot fudge in the cold Delhi winters when my mother used to work two jobs. The halwa was a special treat!
Radhika Viswanathan, Bangalore, India

SERVES 4-6

Preparation: 15 minutes
Cooking: 30 minutes

1 cup / 50 g shredded carrots

1 cup / 240 ml milk or ¾ cup / 180 ml cream

2 tsp each of powdered cinnamon, nutmeg and cloves

3 peppercorns

2 cloves

2-3 tbsp sugar

½ cup / 50 g pistachios or cashews, chopped

1 tbsp sultanas or raisins

3 tbsp oil or ghee

1 Put the shredded carrot and cream/milk with the peppercorns and whole cloves in a saucepan.

2 Bring to a boil, lower the flame to a simmer and slowly cook the milk and carrots together until all the milk/cream is absorbed. Keep stirring to stop the milk and carrots catching on the bottom of the pan. This should take around 25 to 30 minutes; add the sugar and stir to mix in.

3 Remove the peppercorns and cloves from the cooked carrot.

4 In a separate pan, fry the sultanas or raisins and nuts with 1 tablespoon of the oil/ghee and 1 teaspoon of the mixed powdered spices for a few minutes or until the nuts brown slightly. Set aside.

5 Now fry the cooked carrot plus the remaining 1 teaspoon of spices in the remaining oil/ghee. The carrot will turn a deep, rich reddish-brown color.

6 Next, stir in the fried nuts and raisins. Mix well. The fudge or halwa can be eaten hot or cold, alone or with ice cream.

judepics under a CC License

Gooseberry fool

One of my favorite summer desserts. We grow gooseberries in the garden and it's a bit of a tussle as I like them both as this dessert, but also as tangy gooseberry jam. All that topping and tailing is worth it, whichever you go for.

Sistak under a CC license

SERVES 4

Preparation: 20 minutes
Cooking: 10 minutes

2 pounds / 900 g gooseberries, topped and tailed

sugar to taste

2-4 tbsp cream or Greek yogurt

water

1 Place the gooseberries in a heavy pan with water barely to cover the base of the pan. Cook very gently over a low heat – if you cook too high the fruit will catch and burn.

2 Simmer until the gooseberries are soft. Drain and retain the excess liquid (if you add sugar, it makes a nice drink).

3 Let the fruit cool and then, using a hand-held blender, whiz into a smooth mixture. Add sugar to get the sweetness you prefer, and then stir in enough cream or yogurt to make a creamy texture.

4 Leave to cool in the fridge and serve with cream or yogurt, and shortbread cookies.

DESSERTS, DRINKS & CAKES   227

Gramma cake

This dessert is one that's been in my family for three generations, and came from my Russian grandmother. The night before you want the cake, sprinkle the raisins with the baking soda and pour over the boiling water; let it sit overnight.
Lee Bartell, Provincetown, Massachusetts, US

2 cups raisins*

2 tsp baking soda*

2 cups boiling water*

½ cup / 112 g butter

½ cup / 120 g sugar

2 eggs, beaten

2 cups / 300 g wholewheat flour

a few chopped nuts and/or chocolate chips

* soaked together overnight

Heat oven to 325°F/170°C/Gas 3

1 Cream together the butter and sugar. Add the eggs, stirring, and then the flour.

2 Pour the raisin water in and stir to produce a batter-like consistency. Then add the raisins.

3 Now pour the batter into a greased and floured cake pan, sprinkle the chopped nuts and chocolate chips on top, if using, and cook for 45-50 minutes.

4 Leave in the tin for 10-15 minutes to cool before turning out onto a wire rack. If the cake is crumbly, serve from the tin when cool.

Haroset sweetmeats

A Jewish and Moroccan sweetmeat, often served during Pesach/Passover. There is no cooking involved but ideally you should leave it in the fridge for a couple of hours before serving. You can experiment with the ingredients and try different nuts such as pine nuts, almonds and unsalted pistachios.

2 cups / 350 g pitted dates
½ cup / 75 g sultanas
½ cup / 75 g raisins
½ cup / 75 g walnuts
pinch of cinnamon
1-2 tbsp sweet red wine (masala or port)

1 Put the dates, sultanas, raisins, walnuts, cinnamon and half the wine or port in a food processor (a hand-held blender may not be powerful enough). Make a mixture that sticks together, and add a little more wine or port so the mixture binds.

2 Put some waxed paper on a baking sheet.

3 Take small amounts out with a teaspoon and, using clean wet hands, roll them into balls the size of a hazelnut or small walnut. Place these on the baking sheet.

4 Put in the fridge for 2 hours or so.

Ho-ddeock – cinnamon buns

Ho-ddeok is a winter street food in Korea that is slowly transitioning into year-round fare. In essence, it's a fried yeast dumpling, flattened to a pancake, with a sticky cinnamon sugar center – and it's delicious.

Gwangju International Center, via Jacob Lotinga, Gwangju, South Korea

MAKES 6

Preparation: 2 hours (includes time for dough to rise)
Cooking: 10 minutes

1¼ cups / 125 g plain flour

6 tbsp milk

pinch of salt

To start the yeast:

¼ tsp dry yeast

¼ tsp white sugar

2 tbsp water

Filling:

1-2 tsp cinnamon

5 tbsp brown sugar

peanut oil

1 Mix the yeast, white sugar and water and leave in a warm place to ferment for 15 minutes. Sieve the flour into a bowl, add the salt, milk and yeasty water. Mix well, cover and leave to rise for two hours.

2 Mix the cinnamon and brown sugar together for stuffing.

3 Oil your clean hand and take a piece of dough, flatten it with your hand into a circle.

4 Now take a spoonful of the filling and put it in the center of the dough. Form a dumpling by taking up all the sides and then pinching it at the top. Then roll into a ball.

5 Heat up the peanut oil in a frying pan. When hot, put in the filled dumpling ball and flatten it with a spatula. Cook to golden brown, and then flip to cook the other side.

6 When cooked, place the dumplings on a plate with paper towel on it, and serve hot.

Troth Wells

DESSERTS, DRINKS & CAKES   233

Irish barm brack

Is it a bread? Is it a cake? Well, somewhere between the two, which means twice the number of occasions you can eat it. Yum. This is the recipe my mum used to make. She was born in India but had to exchange its sunny climes for rainy Belfast when her parents divorced (all shrouded in secrecy at that time).

It seems that 'brack' could come from 'breac', meaning speckled, referring to the fruit. Barm (often it is pronounced Barn) may come from an old English word 'beorma' meaning yeasty. Another view is that it is a mispronunciation of 'aran', which means bread. Aran Breac would have meant 'speckled bread' – sounds plausible.

Preparation: 15 minutes plus soaking time
Cooking: 60 minutes

1½ cups / 225 g mixed fruit*

½ cup / 100 g soft brown sugar*

¾ cup / 200 ml cold tea*

2 cups / 200 g self-rising flour

1 egg, beaten

pinch of salt

a splash of milk

* soaked together overnight, or for at least 2 hours

Heat oven to 300°F/150°C/Gas 2

1 When ready, sift the flour into a bowl and add the beaten egg, pinch of salt and milk. Mix well.

2 Scoop in the soaked mixed fruit and juices and blend into the flour.

3 Grease and flour the loaf tin and spoon in the mixture.

4 Bake for 1 hour and leave in the tin for 10-15 minutes before turning out to cool.

Mandarin-orange cake

One of our daughters loves to bake and cook. This is her favorite dessert to make for our family... needless to say, we enjoy it very much.

Henriette Faber, Kelowna, British Columbia, Canada

Preparation: 10 minutes
Cooking: 40 minutes

2 cups / 200 g flour

1 cup / 225 g sugar

½ tsp salt

2 tsp baking soda

½ tsp vanilla

4 egg whites

1 can mandarin oranges, drained (retain juice, plus a few slices for decoration)

Pre-heat oven to 350°F/180°C/Gas 4

1 Measure all ingredients in a bowl and mix together. If the mix is a little dry, add 1 tbsp of reserved juice.

2 Pour into greased cake tin and bake for 40 minutes. Turn out to cool and then garnish with a few saved mandarin slices.

Marmalade

This English breakfast favorite uses oranges from sunny Sevilla in southern Spain. According to Kate Colquhoun's book *Taste*, quince pastes were the forerunners of marmalade ('marmelo' is Portuguese for quince) and in the 17th century Rebecca Price – author of *The Compleat Cook* – 'was among the first to make an orange marmalade'. As a kid, I remember when the oranges came in, in January. I hope I helped my mum chop and peel… and then there would be the alluring heady, heavy scent of marmalade cooking.

MAKES: 8-12 JARS

2 pounds / 1 kg Seville (bitter) oranges

1 lemon

1½ quarts / 3 pints water

4 pounds / 2 kg sugar

2 tsp black treacle or molasses

1 Remove the small discs at the stalk ends of the oranges, and clean the fruit. Put the whole oranges and the lemon into a large pan with the water.

2 Cover and bring to the boil, and then simmer gently for about 2 hours until the oranges are tender. Lift them out with a slotted spoon and place on a large plate to cool. Keep the liquid they were cooked in.

3 When the oranges and lemon are cool, cut them in half and scoop out the pulp, pith and pips, keeping the skins. Return the pulp and pips to the cooking water and boil for 5-10 minutes, to extract more pectin that helps set the marmalade.

4 After this, strain off the pulp and pips and measure the liquid. Reduce it to 1½ pints.

5 Next, cut up the peel into the size you prefer.

6 Now put the peel, liquid, sugar and treacle or molasses into a thick-based pan. Stir over a low heat until the sugar dissolves. Then increase the heat and bring to a fast boil. Cook until the setting point is reached (about 15-20 minutes).

7 To test, you can either use a cooking thermometer, or take a small amount on a teaspoon and put on a cold plate. Leave for a few moments and then push gently with your finger. If the marmalade wrinkles against your pressure, then it is setting. If not, continue to boil and test again.

8 When ready, remove the pan from the heat and leave to cool before spooning into clean, warm jam jars.

Mojito

Classic Cuban delight – great on a hot evening.
You can use more soda water if you prefer.

MAKES 2
Preparation: 5 minutes

4 tbsp white rum

1 tbsp lime juice

4 tbsp soda water

½-1 tsp sugar

mint sprig

crushed ice

Place the sugar, lime juice and mint into a glass. Add some of the water and stir to dissolve the sugar. Then put in the rum, ice and remaining soda.

Raspberry daiquiri

Think of this – a really hot summer's day, a bit of a thirst, and lots of beautiful deep red raspberries bursting with flavor. This Cuban cocktail is a treat, and you can use other fruit such as strawberries, peaches or pineapple instead of raspberries. You can also add more juice to make a longer drink, or to make additional servings.

MAKES 3
Preparation: 5 minutes

1 cup / 125 g raspberries

1 cup / 240 ml pineapple juice

½ cup / 120 ml rum

12 ice cubes

2-3 tsp sugar

3 mint leaves

1 Put the ice cubes into a blender to crush them a bit. Then add the other ingredients and whoosh them into a smooth liquid, adding more juice as required.

2 Serve in glasses, decorated with a mint leaf.

Mulled cider

This recipe is from the National Collection of Cider and Perry at Middle Farm, Lewes, in England. We visited on a chilly morning after a brisk seaside walk by the Sussex Downs, and the spicy hot drink was a good accompaniment as we looked at the casks of different ciders, and perries (made from pears) in the collection. Oh, and we tried a few thimblefuls too, of course.

SERVES 4-6

Preparation: 15 minutes
Cooking: 60 minutes

5 cups / 2 liters still, dry cider

3 apples, sliced

2 oranges, sliced

zest and juice of 1 lemon

2 tsp mixed spice

8 whole cloves

2 quills of cinnamon, broken in half

6 tbsp brown sugar

1 Put all the ingredients into a pan, cover and heat gently, without boiling, for at least one hour.

2 'Add friends, fresh from a bracing walk on the Downs, and serve.'

Troth Wells

Papaya/pawpaw cream with cassis liqueur

This one is the very best recipe for making a widely appreciated last-minute dessert. Papayas are found at every corner in Brazil, and are very sweet.
Samantha Teixeira, São Paulo, Brazil (now living in Paris)

SERVES 2-4

Preparation: 10 minutes

1 papaya (ripe/very orange)

4 scoops of vanilla ice cream

Cassis liqueur

1 Remove the seeds from the papaya, peel it and cut it into pieces.

2 Blend the papaya with the ice cream in a blender.

3 Then distribute the papaya cream into individual dishes and pour 1-2 teaspoons of liqueur on top, or as you wish. Serve immediately.

COLOMBIA

Spicy hot chocolate

I drank this on my first night in Colombia's capital, Bogotá, after arriving by myself to stay with friends Adriana and Nick. It means so much because it reminds me of the shock of landing for my first (and only) time in Latin America, and facing temperatures colder than in England – I got to Bogotá in the coldest week they'd had for a long time, and the drink saved me from crying with cold in the middle of July! The chilis, added to the heat and the ginger, saved me from catching cold! For best results, use a chocolatier. This is a small metal jug to heat on the stove with a wooden whisk-style mixer which comes with it... but you can make it without.

Hollie McNish, England

MAKES 1 CUP

Preparation: 2 minutes
Cooking: 5 minutes

cocoa squares*, or dark cooking chocolate

1 cup milk

1-2 tsp fresh ginger, grated

¼ -½ red or green chili, de-seeded and chopped finely

3 tsp cane or brown sugar **

* Such as Mexico's Ibarra, available from specialty shops or www. gourmetsleuth.com Follow instructions.
** Depending on whether you used sweetened chocolate. Adjust to taste.

1 Gently heat the milk until nearly boiling. Then add the cocoa or chocolate squares, the ginger, chopped chili and sugar.

2 Stir until the cocoa squares are melting, then turn down the heat and then, if you are using the chocolatier, 'whisk' with the wooden mixer by placing the handle between your palms and rolling it back and forth. If not using this whisk, just beat gently with a wooden spoon. Do this until the hot chocolate has bubbles and serve at once.

Penny's perfect Aussie Pavlova

Having grown up in Australia, I believe that we created this delicious, light, scrummy dessert. Herbert Sachse, chef of the Hotel Esplanade in Perth, Western Australia, created the pavlova to celebrate the visit of the great Russian ballerina, Anna Pavlova. The meringue shell is crispy on the outside and marshmallowy on the inside. It is lighter than air, as the great ballerina was supposed to be. I know that New Zealanders also lay claim to this delicious dessert and who can blame them – it is so wonderful.

I have been making it for nearly 50 years and am known by family and friends as the Pavlova Queen. So, ENJOY… Stun your guests with a visual then oral sensation! It is the cornflour and lemon juice that makes the yummy marshmallowy/chewy center.
Penny Bassett, Oxford, England

SERVES 4

Preparation: 25 minutes
Cooking: 90 minutes

4 medium egg whites, not chilled *

¾ cup / 150 g caster sugar

1 teaspoon lemon juice or white vinegar

1 teaspoon cornstarch/ cornflour

½ pint cream, whipped

Fruit – anything you like but strawberries look the most amazing; banana and passionfruit taste great.

1 dinner plate covered with baking parchment/ greaseproof paper

* To make a larger pavlova then for every egg white add ¼ cup/50 g sugar, ¼ tsp lemon juice and ¼ tsp cornflour. If I am using 6 egg whites and I only have an electric hand whisk I mix it in 2 bowls.

Heat oven to 300°F/150°C/Gas 2

1 Using a stainless steel or copper bowl (these give best results), whisk egg whites until stiff, gradually add the caster sugar and finally the lemon juice and cornstarch. If you have a very powerful mixer, then the egg whites whip up much more.

2 Spoon the meringue onto the prepared plate, making peaks around the outer edge. This leaves a hollow for the cream and fruit which you put in later.

3 Put onto the middle shelf of the oven and immediately turn down to 275°F/140°C/Gas 1.

4 Cook for about 90 minutes, and then check if the meringue feels crisp in the center. If it does, turn the oven off and leave to cool in the oven, even overnight. If not crisp give it another 15 minutes.

5 When the meringue is cold, fill with the cream and fruit.

Tres leches
– Costa Rican dessert

SERVES 8

Preparation: 15 minutes
Cooking: 40 minutes

½ cup / 110 g sugar ⁺

1 cup / 100 g flour

6 egg yolks, beaten

¾ cup / 180 ml water

1 tsp baking powder

1 tbsp cornstarch

1 cup / 240 ml, plus ¾ cup / 180 ml
whipping cream

1 cup / 240 ml condensed milk

1 cup / 240 ml evaporated milk

pinch of cinnamon

⁺ optional: the condensed milk makes this
very sweet so you may prefer to omit the
sugar.

TIPICAL HOUSE
COSTA RICA
PURA VIDA

I got this recipe from Costa Rica, when I had the privilege to visit that country with my parents in 1992. We had a wonderful stay at a small bed and breakfast in San José, and were very much enjoying the traditional rice and beans, when the cook made a dessert called *Tres leches* (three milks). We tried this cake, and fell in love with it! I asked our waiter if I could get the recipe, and he promptly brought me into the kitchen to meet the cook. She was a kind, plump, 40-ish lady, who didn't speak a word of English. Although I spoke some Spanish, my knowledge did not extend to words for many foods and spices. The cook, the waiter and I sat down together in the kitchen, and with much pantomiming, were able to translate the recipe into English. There was only one word we were having trouble with, and no matter what, we couldn't seem to understand what it was. My mother joined us, and as it turns out, she knew what the mystery ingredient was. She is of Dutch heritage, and recognized the Spanish word for baking powder as very similar to the Dutch word! Anyway, here's the recipe…
Caroline Bartel

EverySpoon under a CC License

Heat oven to 350°F/180°C/Gas 4

1 Put the flour, baking powder and cornstarch into a bowl. Add the egg yolks to the dry ingredients and mix well. Add enough water to make a cake mixture.

2 Transfer into a deep (preferably porcelain or glass) baking dish and bake for 30-40 minutes, or until done and a skewer comes out clean. Leave in the dish to cool.

3 Meanwhile, mix together half of the cream and all of the condensed and evaporated milk in a bowl; then slowly pour this mixture on top of the cake. Leave to stand until the milk mix is absorbed; you can pierce the cake with a skewer or fork to help this process.

4 Beat the remaining whipping cream until thick and spoon on top of the cake before serving. Sprinkle a little cinnamon on top and serve.

INDEX BY REGION AND COURSE

INDEX OF INGREDIENTS & MEAL TYPES